JORDAN
HENDERSON

◆

*NOTES ON
A SEASON*

JORDAN HENDERSON

NOTES ON A SEASON

Reach Sport

www.reachsport.com

First published in Great Britain in 2020 by
Reach Sport, 5 St Paul's Square, Liverpool, L3 9SJ.

www.reachsport.com
@reach_sport

Reach Sport is a part of Reach plc.
One Canada Square, Canary Wharf, London, E15 5AP.

ISBN: 978-1-911613-78-7

Compiled and edited by Chris Brereton

Photographic acknowledgements:
Liverpool FC Getty Images, PA.

Printed and bound by CPI Group (UK) Ltd,
Croydon, CR0 4YY.

NOTES ON A SEASON

2019-20

Introduction: He writes every word...   6

1.   August   11
2.   September   25
3.   October   35
4.   November   59
5.   December   83
6.   January   107
7.   February   127
8.   March   143
      Season halted in its tracks   *156*
9.   June   163
10.   July   181
11.   Inside the dressing room   212
12.   A fitting end...   220

Season statistics   *222*

Introduction

WHAT HE HAS TO SAY IS SIGNIFICANT... AND HE WRITES EVERY WORD HIMSELF

IT has often been said that Jordan Henderson had big boots to fill when he took over from Steven Gerrard as captain of Liverpool Football Club. What never gets mentioned is that he also had Stevie G's Skipper's Notes to fill in the matchday programme.

Compared to leading the Redmen on the pitch and in the dressing-room, perhaps that sounds insignificant, but right from the start of his captaincy, Jordan realised the importance of having a regular opportunity to directly speak to Liverpool supporters.

He not only embraced the responsibility, but took it to a new level by opting to personally write the notes himself. You might think that's standard procedure. It's anything but. Every captain is different. If you try to be a second-rate version of your predecessor you'll never be a first-rate version of yourself and that is particularly significant when following someone like Stevie G.

Gerrard skippered Liverpool for 12 years. Nobody has worn the armband for longer. Gerrard captained the Reds in 473 games. Nobody has worn the armband more often. But he, like most captains, preferred to have his matchday programme column ghost-written.

Before each home game, a colleague would phone Stevie to get his views, turn it into a column written in the first person and email it back to him for approval. Occasionally he'd ask for something to be changed, but that was essentially the process. Not any more.

Initially in 2015, Jordan followed what Stevie had done, but very quickly opted to write every word himself. In my eyes, that gives his column greater gravity as Jordan decides what he writes about rather than responds to questions directing him to discuss particular subjects. What you read is authentic, agenda-free and honest. All I have to do is tidy the odd typo up when he emails his column over, generally two or three days before every home game.

Strict deadlines to ensure programmes are printed and delivered to Anfield on time have to be met, and that applies to the captain of Liverpool FC. If his column is late, it wouldn't be included.

It's my responsibility to ensure he knows when the deadlines are and chase him up if we're getting close to the cut-off point. Which doesn't happen often.

One on occasion, when Jordan was away with the Reds in Europe, he even sent his notes as a text message to meet a deadline when he was unable to forward them by email. That's how committed he is and the content of what he says is also significant.

Henderson is a captain with a social conscience. He focuses on one game at a time on the pitch, but he has a much wider view of Liverpool FC, the challenges facing supporters and society in general.

He understands the sacrifices Liverpool fans make to follow their team. He appreciates the efforts Kopites go to in order to make Anfield the noisy, colourful, emotional, passionate, advantage-giving twelfth man that it is. And he also understands how devastating it was for Kopites not to be there for the title run-in and trophy-lift after winning the Premier League.

Using his notes to highlight all manner of good causes – Alder Hey Children's Hospital, the Owen McVeigh Foundation, Fans Supporting Foodbanks and even Everton's Speedo Mick – makes him a caring captain.

Jordan writes with both perspective and inclusivity. Ensuring the team behind the team are recognised for their endeavours is a regular theme. He genuinely sees everyone as equally important. Even when Jordan was deservedly named as FWA Footballer of the Year for 2020, he wanted it to be viewed as a collective achievement rather than an individual one.

Such an attitude has underpinned Liverpool's success under Jordan's captaincy. You don't become European champions, World champions, Premier League champions – champions of everything – unless you have a truly magnificent captain both on the pitch and in the dressing-room.

Jordan Henderson is that man and whoever eventually replaces him as captain of Liverpool Football Club is going to have big boots to fill. And a matchday programme column to write...

Chris McLoughlin, July 2020

AUG

2019

After leading the team out at Wembley against Manchester City in the Community Shield, Henderson faced a busy month as the Premier League began. It was clear Liverpool would have to get off to a great start if they were to have a season to remember...

9th: Norwich City (PL) H
14th: Chelsea (SC) N
17th: Southampton (PL) A
24th: Arsenal (PL) H
31st: Burnley (PL) A

v Norwich City
Friday, August 9th, 8pm

'I EXPECT US TO WIN EVERY GAME WE GO INTO. WHY WOULDN'T I THINK THAT?'

Premier League

WHEN playing for Liverpool, a new season always brings the questions about expectations before a ball is kicked. It's part and parcel of life as a professional sportsperson and even more so playing for a club like this.

I never have any problem with it, as long as the people asking don't mind getting the same answer. There is no group of people – be it supporters, ex-players, media or pundits – who expect more of this team than we expect of ourselves. It really is that simple.

If, from time to time, we duck giving a specific answer to a question – and by which I mean naming a league position, a particular trophy or, for some of the lads, a goal-scoring or assists target – it's because saying it doesn't make it any more likely to happen. I'm sure players in our dressing-room will have personal targets and many of us will have targets for the team, but setting them publicly doesn't help you achieve them.

I can tell you from a personal standpoint I 'expect' us to win every game we go into. Why wouldn't I think that? Expectations and talk of pressure really don't affect us negatively and it's why being asked about it sometimes leads to non-answers.

Again, speaking for myself, I love the pressure that comes with playing for Liverpool. People have said this summer we might feel less pressure because of what happened last season. For me that just isn't the case.

Whatever happens the previous season, successful or not, is irrelevant when it comes to what you hope to achieve in the coming campaign.

The one element I've found odd, specific to talk of expectations and targets around us, is that there is far too much focus on the domestic season being about just two clubs. I can tell you that no-one in our dressing-room thinks we only have to finish above one side this season to achieve anything – we know full well we will have to be better than 19 other top teams.

Tonight is the perfect example to highlight why the Premier League is so different to other leagues across Europe. The fact is if we don't play well this evening we will likely lose the game because Norwich are a top side with brilliant players.

Other leagues just aren't as competitive throughout as the English top-flight is. People might point to last season and the points gained at the top of the table and the gap, but that doesn't tell the story of the games. There are such tight margins in the Premier League – it makes it so exciting but also unforgiving.

In this league, the moment you're complacent or arrogant you are done for. It's why staying focused and staying hungry is critical and I'm confident as a dressing-room we have those qualities.

Someone showed me a Twitter exchange over the summer that actually captures the mentality we're looking for, not just this coming season but in general. It was a poll by supporters asking to pick the club's greatest ever European night at Anfield. A Liverpool-supporting journalist replied "The. Next. One".

For us that's the focus for this season – on to the next one. But for us that mantra isn't about just European nights or trophies and titles in general, it's about each and every match we play.

Starting this evening, there is only one achievement possible for us and that's to win this football game. Our mindset is the only game that matters is the next one we play. So all of our ambitions and all our expectations are centred on Norwich City at Anfield tonight.

The maximum you can win in each moment is the game you're playing, so that's our target. We know we need to be at our best. We know we face a tough battle to achieve it.

As a team we want our supporters to dream and dream big. At Wembley the passion and noise from the Liverpool fans was magnificent. They showed the right mentality – when Liverpool play it always matters. They gave everything to make the atmosphere special and it made a difference to us and how we attacked the game. The supporters who went to Wembley helped set the tone. For each game, give everything you have.

We want everyone to have the biggest ambitions possible. It's our job to deliver and to do that we can't afford distraction and we can't afford to pause and feel satisfaction. What we achieved last season will be cherished by everyone connected to this club forever, not least myself. But now, for us as a group of players, we're already focused on 2019/20.

Quite simply we have to be if we want to have a chance of success again.

What we can afford is to keep the focus on what's ahead and what we can positively affect.

The. Next. One.

Liverpool 4, Norwich City 1

Goals: Hanley (7og), Salah (19), Van Dijk (28), Origi (42)

Line-up (4-3-3): Alisson (Adrian 39), Alexander-Arnold, Gomez, Van Dijk, Robertson, Fabinho, Henderson (c), Wijnaldum, Salah, Firmino (Milner 86), Origi (Mane 74). Subs not used: Keita, Oxlade-Chamberlain, Shaqiri, Matip

Jordan's post-match reaction: 'It was the start of the Premier League, we wanted to go out and start really well, which we managed to do. We just want to concentrate on our performance levels, consistency. We're a very hungry set of lads that want to improve all the time and get success.'

Captain's contribution

Henderson set the tone for the season, demonstrating incredible stamina, willingness to chase every loose ball and he even filled in at right-back for a short time.

Wednesday, August 14th, 8pm
UEFA Super Cup,
Liverpool 2, Chelsea 2 (after extra time, Liverpool win 5-4 on penalties)
Besiktas Arena

Goals: Mane (48, 95)

Line-up (4-3-3): Adrian, Gomez, Matip, Van Dijk, Robertson (Alexander-Arnold 90), Fabinho, Henderson (c), Milner (Wijnaldum 64), Salah, Mane (Origi 103), Oxlade-Chamberlain (Firmino 45). Subs not used: Lonergan, Kelleher, Lallana, Shaqiri, Brewster, Hoever, Elliott

Jordan's post-match reaction: 'We're delighted for Adri, who has just come to the club and he's the hero again tonight. He's come in, he's been asked a lot, but he's done a great job and hopefully that's just the start. It was a tough game, Chelsea are a good side. It's not a nice way to lose [penalties], we know that after the Community Shield, but we're delighted we've won this one We want to win as many trophies as we can.'

Captain's contribution

Henderson lifted Liverpool's fourth UEFA Super Cup after a relatively quiet, yet effective, game in midfield. The Liverpool captain drove his side on and was thrilled to be picking up more silverware for the Reds.

Saturday, August 17th, 3pm
Premier League
Southampton 1, Liverpool 2

Goals: Mane (45+1), Firmino (71)

Line-up (4-3-3): Adrian, Alexander-Arnold, Matip, Van Dijk, Robertson, Wijnaldum, Milner (c) (Fabinho 74), Oxlade-Chamberlain (Henderson 89), Mane, Firmino, Salah (Origi 79). Subs not used: Lonergan, Gomez, Lallana, Shaqiri

Alex Oxlade-Chamberlain made his first league start since April 2018 following a serious knee injury and was thrilled to be back involved. He said: 'I'm delighted that I could help contribute to the team because that's what I've missed so much, being able to contribute and help this set of players to achieve things. It was really nice to be back out there. We didn't want to come off the pitch with any excuses as to why we didn't get the right result. We suffered in patches but we managed to come through them, which we knew was going to happen. We played some really good stuff in parts as well.'

Captain's contribution

Henderson came off the bench with just a minute to go as Jürgen Klopp looked to freshen his midfield options in a bid to hang on to Liverpool's precious advantage. It worked.

v Arsenal
Saturday, August 24th, 5.30pm

'IF ANYONE DESERVES PRAISE FOR PERFORMING AT THE HIGHEST LEVEL REPEATEDLY, IT'S OUR FANS'

Premier League

IT'S fair to say some of the most exciting games I've been involved in since joining Liverpool have been against Arsenal.

I'm not sure what it is about this fixture that brings out the best in both teams, but at the end of the 90 minutes you always feel like you've been part of a great contest. And it's not always about games with a high scoreline either, even though there have been a few in the Premier League era. It's more to do with the intensity of the game.

The away match in London last season, that finished 1-1, was one of the most relentless I've witnessed. I wasn't involved that day but I was watching it obviously and it was exhausting enough doing that.

It's hard for me to put my finger on why the games pan out as they do, but from our perspective the respect we have for them as a team and club couldn't be any higher. They go into every game determined to play their way and impose themselves on the opposition. We know they'll focus on their strengths and getting at us every chance they have.

Also, every Arsenal side I have faced in my career so far – and I'm sure this one is no different – always has world-class players throughout. Players with the mindset to be positive at all times.

When you face Arsenal you know that your own commitment and concentration has to be at its maximum for the entire game. If you drop even half a percent they will punish you. They've started the season strongly and we know nothing less than our absolute maximum will be required tonight if we're to get the result we want.

Continuing with an Arsenal link as such, it was magic for all of us to see Alex Oxlade-Chamberlain make his first Premier League start in 16 months at Southampton at the weekend.

It's testimony to Ox as a person and a pro that the lads at Arsenal who worked with him still speak of him in the highest possible terms.

If you know Ox it's easy to understand why people love him so much.

I've spoken enough about how he conducted himself and still supported the team during his rehab process, but I think last weekend probably was an important milestone to pass. Having got that start under his belt, we can now focus on the impact and contribution he'll have on our season and future seasons. Of course patience is still important, though.

Ox will be the first to say he hasn't scratched the surface of his potential for what he can do for us and I'm sure there will be times in the coming days, weeks and months when he'll still be feeling his way back.

But it was hard not to be excited seeing him at St Mary's last week and as a player it is contributing on the pitch that always feels the most important thing.

Speaking of contribution, on behalf of all the players I want to recognise what an impact Liverpool supporters have had at the start of this season.

As a team we know it's unrealistic to be at our best at the very beginning of a campaign, as much as we want to be. The gaffer has always said if your best games of the season are the first ones then you probably won't be having the most impressive of campaigns. But our fans have been on it since day one – and to be honest it's really helped the team through games.

Liverpool supporters dominated the occasion at Wembley in the Community Shield, made Anfield bounce against Norwich, took over three-quarters of the stadium in Istanbul and were in incredible voice at Southampton.

Around the Istanbul and Southampton trips a lot was made of the impact on the players and how tiredness could play a part. Let's have it right. We travel in luxury and are looked after unbelievably well whereas the supporters fork out huge sums of money to follow us.

I know the travelling element is far from straightforward; early starts, long days and late nights just to be able to get to and from our games.

So if anyone deserves praise for performing at the highest level repeatedly, despite a hectic schedule, it's our fans. As a team we are and will always be grateful.

Liverpool 3, Arsenal 1

Goals: Matip (41), Salah (49 pen, 58)

Line-up (4-3-3): Adrian, Alexander-Arnold, Matip, Van Dijk, Robertson, Henderson (c), Fabinho, Wijnaldum (Milner 69), Salah, Firmino (Lallana 86), Mane (Oxlade-Chamberlain 77). Subs not used: Kelleher, Gomez, Shaqiri, Origi

Jordan's post-match reaction: 'Another three points against a good side, a good performance – so, overall, delighted with the game. They started really well and won both their games so we knew it would be difficult. But we knew if we did the right things, played to our strengths, defended really well and were clinical in front of goal, then we'd hurt them. We managed to do that, so overall it was a really good performance. If we want to be really critical, we're disappointed with the [Arsenal] goal – I should have cleared it on the edge of the box. But we've got to be delighted with the three points, it's tough in the Premier League. [It was] another great performance. All three goals were really good. Now we need to recover well, train hard this week and prepare for a tough game against Burnley.'

Captain's contribution

Another breathless performance from Liverpool's captain who looked full of energy when he came out of the tunnel and displayed that same intensity from start to finish. He harassed Arsenal's midfield all game and was a powerful, vocal presence.

Saturday, August 31st, 5.30pm
Premier League
Burnley 0, Liverpool 3

Goals: Wood (33og), Mane (37), Firmino (80)

Line-up (4-3-3): Adrian, Alexander-Arnold, Matip, Van Dijk, Robertson, Wijnaldum, Fabinho, Henderson (c) (Oxlade-Chamberlain 71), Salah, Firmino (Origi 85), Mane (Shaqiri 85). Subs not used: Kelleher, Milner, Gomez, Lallana

Jordan's post-match reaction: 'We worked extremely hard defensively to win second balls, which is important against Burnley. The two strikers [Chris Wood and Ashley Barnes] are really physical. I thought we coped with them really well. Going forward we looked good at times and scored some brilliant goals. We want to continue that form, keep doing the right things, keep working hard as a team. If we do that, we can put on performances like that.'

Captain's contribution

Henderson continued to play as an attacking midfielder rather than sitting more defensively and he again proved why Jürgen Klopp has so much faith in him. He was tireless in attack and defence, produced some wonderful balls into the box and continued his really bright and buoyant start to the season.

SEP

2019

The Reds were off to a flier and Henderson had already lifted the first silverware of the season. After the international break, September would bring more challenges, at home and abroad...

14th: Newcastle United (PL) H
17th: Napoli (CL) A
22nd: Chelsea (PL) A
25th: MK Dons (CC) A
28th: Sheffield United (PL) A

Jordan Henderson

v Newcastle United
Saturday, September 14th, 12.30pm

'I'M PRETTY SURE I HOLD THE RECORD FOR HANDING OVER MAN OF THE MATCH AWARDS'

Premier League

FINDING out who we are facing in the Champions League group stage was a little different this year because we were training at the time of the draw, so it wasn't until we came back that we discovered who we'd be taking on.

Under usual circumstances that would be cause for excitement enough, but there were a couple of added reasons why we were all so keen to find out what was happening at the ceremony in Monaco.

I can't begin to tell you how chuffed we all were for Alisson Becker and Virgil van Dijk for winning in the awards categories they were nominated in. Big Ali scooped UEFA Champions League Keeper of the Season and Virg won Defender of the Season and, of course, the Men's Player of the Year.

What was typical of both players – and typical of the attitude in our team – is that they were quick to say the prizes were as much down to the help of everyone at the club as anything else, not just themselves.

I'm sure when some people hear that sort of thing they roll their eyes and think 'well you would say that in public', but both of these lads epitomise our dressing-room by not just saying it but meaning it.

Both Ali and Virg have been as generous in private as they have been in public to make sure everyone who supports us on a day-to-day basis feels part of moments like these.

It's why, when Virgil's name was announced on stage for the main award of the ceremony, there was a huge cheer that went up around Melwood from those who'd headed up to the canteen as soon as they'd come in to try and find out what was going on in Monaco.

It was a really nice moment and it prompted an inevitable scramble of iPhones to say congratulations, but every person inside our training ground that day was pleased as punch.

Individual awards within team sports are an interesting topic, but I don't think it ever causes anything but happiness for the wider group when the situation at a club is a healthy one.

I'm pretty sure I hold the record for handing over man-of-the-match awards to team-mates during post-match interviews, but even though I might have joked about it before, I couldn't care less who I'm giving it to – as long as they're wearing our shirt and we've won the game.

I mentioned before about both Ali and Virg being quick to praise 'the team' for their individual wins that night, but what is even more important is the other part of what both said.

Both of them – and I know this to be 100 per cent true – would trade any individual honours for more team prizes.

The more 'Player of the Year' awards our guys are winning in football can only be a good thing, because more often that not it means the team itself has achieved something.

Later this month Ali, Virg and the gaffer, Jürgen, are up for FIFA awards and I hope they win them.

But I know all three would swap them in a heartbeat for three league points. It's great that we have a culture where we can appreciate the happiness of the individual knowing all the time that the group is what matters to them and us the most.

Finally, although I'm conscious these words coming from a committed Mackem might not do him any favours, on a personal level I'd like to say how fantastic it is to see Steve Bruce back in the Premier League.

I owe Steve and the staff he had with him at Sunderland a great deal and I'll always be grateful for what he, and they, did for me and my career.

Andy Robertson will back me up when I say there are few managers in the game today who are appreciated and respected by the players who have played under him as much as Steve.

He helped me become a better football player and a better person. Robbo says exactly the same about himself.

Clearly I hope Steve leaves Anfield disappointed today, but I know he'll have a successful season and do very well at Newcastle because he's a brilliant leader of a football team and club.

Liverpool 3, Newcastle United 1

Goals: Mane (28, 40), Salah (72)

*Line-up (4-3-3): Adrian, Alexander-Arnold, Matip, Van Dijk (c),
Robertson, Oxlade-Chamberlain (Milner 75), Fabinho, Wijnaldum
(Shaqiri 84), Salah, Mane, Origi (Firmino 37). Subs not used:
Kelleher, Gomez, Henderson, Lallana*

*Andy Robertson had a brilliant game for the Reds and praised
the way Liverpool got back into the match. He said: 'Here, we've
not been behind very often so it was a good reaction because
sometimes when it doesn't happen very often, people can be a bit
stunned by it – players and fans. Everyone reacted really well
and luckily we got back on level terms because the longer the
game goes, Steve Bruce's game plan comes in; I've been a part
of it and I know how good they are at it. Luckily we got on
level terms quite quickly. We're gutted for big Div coming off –
hopefully it's not too serious. But to bring Bobby on is always a
nice sub to have. Obviously he came back late from internationals
and the manager decided to put him on the bench. When he came
on he showed his class and could probably have had three or four
assists. He had a big impact and that's what we needed. Luckily
we had enough for the three points.'*

Captain's contribution

Henderson was not required against Newcastle as
Jürgen Klopp rested his captain for the hectic schedule
ahead.

Tuesday, September 17th, 8pm
UEFA Champions League,
Napoli 2, Liverpool 0

Line-up (4-3-3): Adrian, Alexander-Arnold, Matip, Van Dijk, Robertson, Fabinho, Milner (Wijnaldum 66), Henderson (c) (Shaqiri 87), Firmino, Mane, Salah. Subs not used: Kelleher, Lovren, Gomez, Oxlade-Chamberlain, Lallana

Jordan's post-match reaction: 'At home Napoli are a good side and they are going to create some good chances. You've got to be prepared to defend as a team, which I felt we did. We won some great balls in midfield and counter-attacked really well, but it was just that last little bit – and obviously the mistakes for the goals – that we need to improve on. Overall, we can be better of course. We'll take responsibility, we'll move forward and try to react in the right way.'

Captain's contribution

Henderson had a quiet night against the Italian side as Liverpool laboured against Napoli. The Liverpool captain's work-rate was as outstanding as always but he could not help unlock Napoli's defence on a difficult evening for the Reds.

Sunday, September 22nd, 4.30pm
Premier League
Chelsea 1, Liverpool 2

Goals: Alexander-Arnold (14), Firmino (30)

Line-up (4-3-3): Adrian, Alexander-Arnold, Matip, Van Dijk, Robertson, Wijnaldum, Fabinho, Henderson (c) (Lallana 84), Salah (Gomez 90+2), Firmino, Mane (Milner 71). Subs not used: Kelleher, Oxlade-Chamberlain, Shaqiri, Brewster

Trent Alexander-Arnold scored his first of the season against Chelsea and was determined to go one better than last year in the Premier League. He said: 'Losing the title was the worst feeling many of us had ever felt in football. Coming so close to feeling as though you have made something of yourself and made your family proud and then in a split second, you feel as if you have let everyone down in the world, you feel as if you weren't good enough. It's something we talked about straight away after the end of last season. It's motivation not to feel that way again.'

Captain's contribution

This was more like it from Liverpool and Henderson as the Reds put the disappointment of Napoli behind them with a fine showing at Stamford Bridge. Henderson was superb, working his socks off to earn a victory at one of the toughest away grounds in the Premier League.

Wednesday, September 25th, 7.45pm
Carabao Cup third round
MK Dons 0, Liverpool 2

Goals: Milner (41), Hoever (69)

Line-up (4-3-3): Kelleher, Hoever (Van den Berg 90+2), Gomez, Lovren, Milner (c), Jones, Keita (Chirivella 63), Lallana, Oxlade-Chamberlain (Kane 82), Brewster, Elliott. Subs not used: Lonergan, Lewis, Longstaff, Clarkson

James Milner stepped in and captained after Jürgen Klopp rotated his squad and the veteran midfielder did a typically classy job of steering Liverpool's youngsters through the match. He said: 'It's always tough when you have a mixture of guys who haven't played many minutes and a group of youngsters, but you could see the style of football we wanted to play. When you look at how good our squad is, it's not easy for the youngsters to get to the level they need to be, but they've shown they want to get better and better. Everyone is pushing, and that's what the senior boys need: competition for places.'

Captain's contribution

Henderson was given a well-deserved night off as the next generation of Liverpool stars were entrusted with producing the goods in the Carabao Cup.

Jordan Henderson

Saturday, September 28th, 12.30pm
Premier League
Sheffield United 0, Liverpool 1

Goal: Wijnaldum (70)

Line-up (4-3-3): Adrian, Alexander-Arnold, Matip, Van Dijk, Robertson, Henderson (c) (Origi 64), Fabinho, Wijnaldum, Salah, Firmino (Milner 87), Mane (Oxlade-Chamberlain 90+4). Subs not used: Kelleher, Lovren, Gomez, Lallana

Gini Wijnaldum was the difference on the day, sealing the three points and was delighted with the way Liverpool have started the season. He said: 'They play with a lot of passion. Their fighting spirit was really good and when they had space they played football. We wanted to create chances but I think they defended really good. But all that matters is we have the three points. Especially at the early stage of the season, you have to make sure that you collect as many points as possible because normally during the season you get better and better.'

Captain's contribution

Henderson returned to the side for the difficult trip to Bramall Lane and Chris Wilder's side made it tough for Liverpool's midfield. Henderson was Liverpool's heartbeat, looking to win every loose ball before he was replaced by Divock Origi in the second half.

OCT

2019

Liverpool had a month containing six matches in three competitions. After such an impressive start to the season, it was vital they maintained their momentum - and their winning ways...

2nd: Salzburg (CL) H
5th: Leicester City (PL) H
20th: Manchester United (PL) A
23rd: KRC Genk (CL) A
27th: Tottenham Hotspur (PL) H
30th: Arsenal (CC) H

Jordan Henderson

'IT WAS BRUTAL IN TRUTH, COMING ON IN A GAME WE'D GO ON TO LOSE 5-0'

UEFA Champions League

THE thing that struck me most watching and supporting the team in the Carabao Cup against MK Dons last week was the importance of experience and youthful freshness for a modern-day squad.

Our two goalscorers on the night highlight it. The second was from a brilliant header from our 17-year-old Dutch defender Ki-Jana Hoever. But our first was from... well... a slightly older James Milner.

As is always the case, the focus on the night fell mainly on the younger stars, because it was a first opportunity for many watching to see them in that sort of environment.

We were all buzzing for Curtis Jones to pick up the MOTM award, particularly knowing how much it will have meant to him being a local lad. Well-deserved as well – he was brilliant. But I think Curt would be the first to admit there were plenty of decent candidates for it on the night.

To see Harvey Elliott play as maturely and as confidently as he did, aged just 16, was tremendous. And Caoimhin Kelleher produced a couple of worldie saves to show why he's so highly thought of.

In terms of competitive senior debuts for Liverpool I think I'm right in saying there were five on the night: Caoimhin and Harvey, as already mentioned, along with Rhian Brewster, Herbie Kane and Sepp van den Berg. We're delighted for all five of them as making your debut for a club like Liverpool is always special, and to do it with a win was a magnificent effort.

However, people shouldn't ignore the role and guidance of the more senior lads. I'll be truthful, playing in situations like that isn't easy – in fact, it's outright hard. The gaffer said so himself.

It's a group that haven't played together before, so the responsibility on the experienced guys to help the team through it is so important and underlines how lucky we are to have the professionals we do in our team. In games like that you can't just worry about yourself and none of our lads did that.

The boys provided superb leadership for the teenage lads and I know they'd have all appreciated it and benefited from it.

Every footballer with an appearance under their belt has the same thing in common: we've all made a debut. I remember mine, also as a teenager. It was brutal in truth, coming on as a sub for Sunderland in a game we'd go on to lose 5-0. But even with that disappointment I'll never forget the help and support of senior players in and around that time.

Funnily enough my competitive debut for Liverpool came against Sunderland and again, even with a fair number of senior appearances to my name, it was important to have support from my team-mates during that match.

What's important for the young lads now is to take

all the positive energy from that experience and use it to drive on. The Academy set-up at Liverpool is world-class and it makes sure the young lads know how to make a career in this industry. Be it for Liverpool or another club, you need to have total commitment each and every day.

What better person to look to than James Milner, leading the team out at MK Dons, as a living, breathing example of it?

I mentioned Curtis picking up the man-of-the-match award last Wednesday for the first team. It was brilliant to hear on Saturday, after we'd played and won at Sheffield United, that Curt had followed that up with two goals for the Under-23s against Arsenal.

That's the attitude needed. Whether it be the first team or the 23s or the 18s, give total commitment when you play for your club at whatever level.

Away from the pitch, the highlight of the week has undoubtedly been the Steps4Stephen walk, which finished at Anfield on Sunday.

The 167-mile walk started off a few days earlier at Bradford City and, if I'm honest, I get tired just thinking about it so I can only imagine what it was like for the participants, especially as they had to cope with some terrible weather along the way.

Everyone who took part was supporting Stephen Darby and the Darby Rimmer Foundation to raise vital funds for research into Motor Neurone Disease.

As a club, we will stand shoulder-to-shoulder with Stephen, but what the walkers did went well above the call of duty and I take my hat off to each and every one of them.

If anyone is able to support their efforts the fundraising page is still open and can be found at justgiving.com/crowdfunding/steps4stephen.

Liverpool 4, Salzburg 3

Goals: Mane (9), Robertson (25), Salah (36, 69)

Line-up (4-3-3): Adrian, Alexander-Arnold, Gomez, Van Dijk, Robertson, Henderson (c) (Milner 62), Fabinho, Wijnaldum (Origi 64), Salah (Keita 90), Firmino, Mane. Subs not used: Kelleher, Lovren, Oxlade-Chamberlain, Lallana

Mo Salah scored two goals and was Liverpool's stand-out performer on yet another thrilling European night at Anfield. He said: 'I think they had a good game and after they scored three goals it becomes difficult, but we play again to win the Champions League, we focus on each game. I think when we were winning 3-0 we needed to score a fourth and fifth.'

Captain's contribution

Henderson's vision and passing range came to the fore in the first half as he frequently launched Liverpool's attacks and closed down Salzburg's midfield. He was replaced by James Milner in the second half.

v Leicester City
Saturday, October 5th, 3pm

'I WILL ALWAYS BE GRATEFUL TO SIR KENNY FOR HAVING ENOUGH BELIEF IN ME'

Premier League

THERE is little room for sentiment in football and today I have no doubt at all that the manager in the away dugout will have as much desire to win here as we all have in looking to beat his side.

That said, it's impossible to ignore the person, along with key staff members, returning to Anfield this afternoon for the first time since they left Liverpool.

For 90-plus minutes we are opponents, but the only way to describe Brendan Rodgers, Kolo Toure, Chris Davies and Glen Driscoll is as returning friends – and as people who did a lot to help not just this club as a whole but a number of individual players within it, myself included. I know they'll get a warm welcome before and after the game.

I will always be grateful to Sir Kenny Dalglish for having enough belief in myself to bring me here in the first place. But as well as Sir Kenny, Brendan played a massive part in my Liverpool career and development as a player here.

It's already apparent that Brendan is doing for the Leicester players what he did for us when he came to Liverpool. It's obvious how much the lads there have bought into what he and his staff are looking to create and achieve, and it's genuinely no surprise to me that they've made such a positive start to this season.

In the three years-plus I spent working for Brendan I learned so much from him. He was massively generous when it came to giving time to explain what he wanted from you, in terms of improvement and development. I mentioned the faith Sir Kenny showed in offering me the chance to become a Liverpool player, and I have the same appreciation to Brendan for making me captain. I was still relatively young at that time and I'm sure there would have been 'safer' choices to make.

That he chose to hand me the armband sums up the impact Brendan had here: he made us all believe in ourselves and push ourselves to be better.

It's fantastic to see Kolo working by his side now as well and I'm sure the supporters will be made up to see him back at Anfield. When you share a dressing-room with Kolo as a team-mate, it isn't hard to see why he achieved so much in his career as a player. His standards were unbelievably high and he was always keen to help the other lads.

It's no surprise he's become a coach now – and a successful one with Brendan – because you could tell as a player he had both that knowledge about the game and the ability to explain it and pass it on.

Chris Davies and Glen Driscoll were key members of Brendan's staff while at Liverpool too and have remained just as important to him at Celtic and Leicester. Both were massively respected by the players during their time with us and again, it's great to see them doing well and playing such a big part in Brendan's success.

Of course, as I pointed out right at the beginning, friendships are on hold for the game itself. I know all four well enough to know they'll be desperate to come here and get a result. Not because it's about making a point to Liverpool, but because everything they do is about getting the best results for their team.

That team is now Leicester City, but they'll come up against a team who are also desperate for the result, as we always are regardless of who or where we play. Today is no different. There are three more points up for grabs, we want them and we'll do everything we can to try and get them.

Finally, given after this match we have a two-week break from domestic football for the internationals, I want to mention Trent Alexander-Arnold, who will turn 21 years old in the next few days.

It's incredible to think he's still that young, as it feels like he's been part of the team now for ages, although it does only seem like yesterday when this quiet, shy, unassuming boy joined us at Melwood for training sessions. Back then he was nicknamed 'The Pup,' but I know it's not a name we can or would want to use anymore given how much he's developed both as a player and a person since those early days.

When you think about what he's already achieved, at a club like this one where competition is so fierce, it's frightening really. The thing with Trent, though, is that not only has all the success and recognition not changed him, it never will.

His determination and will to win at everything he does is astonishing. Obviously when it comes to things like table-tennis and playing other games like that he's miles off it compared to me...but bless him, he keeps trying.

Joking aside, Trent has the perfect attitude for a modern-day player and he will be at this level for a very, very long time because he has the talent and the attitude to make sure he doesn't take a backwards step.

Liverpool 2, Leicester City 1

Goals: Mane (40), Milner (90+5 pen)

Line-up (4-3-3): Adrian, Alexander-Arnold, Lovren, Van Dijk, Robertson, Wijnaldum (Henderson 78), Fabinho, Milner (c), Salah (Lallana 90), Mane, Firmino (Origi 78). Subs not used: Kelleher, Keita, Gomez, Elliott

James Milner grabbed a late winner for Liverpool. He said: 'We're just delighted to get the win; it was always going to be tough, they're a good team. We looked pretty tired in the second half but we found a way to win again.'

Captain's contribution

Henderson started the game on the bench but came on with 12 minutes remaining to help the Reds find the winner. His celebrations at the final whistle underlined how desperate he was to win the match.

Jordan Henderson

Sunday, October 20th, 4.30pm
Premier League
Manchester United 1, Liverpool 1

Goal: Lallana (85)

Line-up (4-3-3): Alisson, Alexander-Arnold, Matip, Van Dijk, Robertson, Wijnaldum (Keita 82), Fabinho, Henderson (c) (Lallana 71), Origi (Oxlade-Chamberlain 60), Firmino, Mane. Subs not used: Adrian, Lovren, Gomez, Milner

Jordan's post-match reaction: 'I'm delighted for Adam, because he's worked so hard and he deserves that. He saved us today and that could be a big point come the end of the season. I didn't think we performed well enough in the first half, not our usual selves really, especially with the ball. We could have been a lot better but I thought second half was a lot better. We changed it a little bit tactically, which helped us, and I thought the longer the game went on we were pushing for that winner, and towards that last five to 10 minutes I thought we were going to get it. When you can't win, you don't lose, and that's the sign of a good team.'

Captain's contribution

Henderson loves the big occasions and was vocal and strong at Old Trafford, helping to restrict the home side to very few chances.

Wednesday, October 23rd, 8pm
UEFA Champions League,
KRC Genk 1, Liverpool 4

Goals: Oxlade-Chamberlain (2, 57), Mane (77), Salah (87)

Line-up (4-3-3): Alisson, Milner, Lovren, Van Dijk, Robertson (Gomez 63), Oxlade-Chamberlain (Wijnaldum 74), Fabinho, Keita, Salah, Firmino (Origi 80), Mane. Subs not used: Adrian, Henderson, Lallana, Brewster

Alex Oxlade-Chamberlain continued his impressive form and again proved that his serious knee injury was now firmly consigned to the past. Two goals and a commanding performance helped his confidence to soar even higher. He said: 'It's nice to be back out there. It's a special tournament to play in, a competition we all grew up wanting to play in one day. It's inspirational, it's something I've wanted to get back to do. It's just nice to be back in the starting line-up and try to put in a performance to help the team. To get a few goals was a bonus. We saw that we have a lot to improve, but we're getting results, which is good.'

Captain's contribution

With Liverpool looking comfortable in the Champions League, Jürgen Klopp saw an opportunity to rest Henderson and he watched from the substitutes bench as the Reds ran out easy winners.

Jordan Henderson

v Tottenham Hotspur
Sunday, October 27th, 4.30pm

'I AM BUZZING - AND I'M SURE THERE'S A LOT MORE TO COME AS THIS SEASON DEVELOPS'

Premier League

I WOULD struggle to name a tougher opponent we faced last season in all competitions than Tottenham Hotspur.

It can often be the case that only looking at results, rather than how they were achieved, means you can be fooled into a false narrative. Yes, we won all three games against Spurs last season – but that doesn't even begin to tell the story.

At Wembley the match hung in the balance until the final whistle, because they kept coming and coming and refused to accept defeat. We were definitely pleased to hear the whistle go at the end. The Anfield game was settled with a stoppage-time winner that even the most biased Red would have to admit needed some good fortune. And the Madrid game was alive before the 87th minute when Divock scored and it remained alive even after that.

Tottenham are a team that are admired by everyone in the Premier League and now across Europe and it's not hard to see why. World-class players, with a manager who has a clear style and approach they all believe in.

A number of today's visitors are team-mates for me, as well as opponents. As with all the England lads in our team, we are good friends with our fellow countrymen who'll be in the away dressing-room today.

When we're away we do inevitably speak about club football and you can see how hungry the Spurs lads are to go even better this season, after achieving so much last.

We can all definitely identify with that feeling: having a great season, coming close and then coming back to go again.

No one here is being distracted by the so called 'issues' which Tottenham have had early on. We know they're an even better side than the one who can rightly call themselves one of Europe's elite after the last campaign. They've strengthened in the transfer market and they have that spirit and belief in each other that comes from being together for such a long time.

I don't think the results from last season will be a motivating factor in this game today, but my personal experience is that these games are unbelievably intense regardless. They're a squad of competitors and so are we.

The games are also usually hectic and tense but of really high quality. We have to be ready to fight and scrap until the very last kick of the match.

I think whatever happens both sides have a healthy respect for each other and that usually shows on the pitch when the game is done. We respect their strengths and I think it's fair to say they acknowledge ours.

It wouldn't be accurate to say we 'enjoy' these games because when you're playing in them that's almost impossible. But it's a fixture that now has added significance each season because as clubs we compete with each other on all fronts.

Finally, I couldn't not mention Adam Lallana for his match-saving moment at Old Trafford last week or Alex Oxlade-Chamberlain for his magic in Genk.

It's no secret how close Adam and I are – as are our families. It wasn't just the goal that lit up Manchester for us, it was his entire performance. The truth is we've seen that quality day-in and day-out at Melwood for a very long time.

He's as fit and as strong as I've ever known him. If anything he's getting quicker in mind and that is reflected in how influential he can be in games.

Those of us who've seen Adam over the past 18 months specifically know he's been fit, available and contributing through the quality he brings to our squad every day in training.

And on Ox: two goals midweek and the second of those was a 'wow' moment. I was warming up on the touchline when he scored it and after I picked my jaw off the floor, I couldn't do anything but clap. That's such a difficult technique to pull off, but it is typical Ox.

Those goals will give him a big boost I'm sure, not that he really needed it though. He's a massive personality and someone whose quality is going to be so valuable.

I'm buzzing for both of them and I'm sure there is so much more to come as this season develops.

I'm sure the atmosphere will be big at Anfield today because it's a big, big game. We will need the crowd to be the wind at our backs. I think games like this – with two great teams and clubs – deserve special energy in the ground and I know we will get it. Hopefully we can reward our fans with a contest to enjoy.

Liverpool 2, Tottenham Hotspur 1

Goals: Henderson (52), Salah (75 pen)

Line-up (4-3-3): Alisson, Alexander-Arnold, Lovren, Van Dijk, Robertson, Henderson (c), Fabinho, Wijnaldum (Milner 77), Salah (Gomez 85), Firmino (Origi 90), Mane. Subs not used: Adrian, Keita, Oxlade-Chamberlain, Lallana

Jordan's post-match reaction: 'The crowd was unbelievable again and kept us going right until the end – that was important. The performance was good and the chances we created were very good; the keeper made some top saves. We kept going, showed great mentality and deservedly got the three points. It's always nice to score, especially at Anfield in front of the Kop. It was to get us back in the game, which was important. The performance was brilliant from the lads, we deserved the three points.'

Captain's contribution

A refreshed Henderson drew Liverpool level after Harry Kane's early opener and was a thorn in Spurs' side all day. His left-footed finish at the Kop end gave his team the platform to go on and win the game.

v Arsenal
Wednesday, October 30th, 7.30pm

'ALI WOULD BE THE FIRST TO TELL YOU THAT KEEPERS ARE A 'TEAM WITHIN A TEAM"

Carabao Cup

IT'S been great to see Alisson Becker return to the side so seamlessly and without drama. Massive credit must go to the big man for that.

We all know how important Ali was for us last season in all competitions and that's been reflected in the recognition he's received over the course of this year. It's all well-deserved and everyone at Melwood – and I am sure among our fanbase – is delighted for him.

But Ali would be the first to tell you that keepers are a 'team within the team' and the contribution of the others is absolutely critical to maintaining high standards. Without those around him, Ali, I'm sure, would say he wouldn't be able to perform at the elite level he does so consistently.

When we said goodbye and good luck to Simon Mignolet in August it was pretty clear whoever came in had a tough act to follow. But Adrian has been absolutely amazing for us – on and off the field. They were big shoes to fill, but he's filled them and then some.

Even leaving aside the match-winning performances on the pitch, in the dressing-room it feels like he's never been anywhere else but with us. His personality reflects how he plays: positive, brave, alert, team first and individual second. Just like Simon, he's every inch a 'number one' and as outfield players it's huge to know we have someone like him in our squad.

Another summer addition in the keeping department

that maybe went under the radar was Andy Lonergan, but again he's been brilliant for us. 'Lonners' initially came as a training keeper to help us out pre-season but settled instantly. His performances in the USA were top-drawer, but in training he's kept us as outfield players on our toes.

The lads were absolutely made up when that short-term deal was made into a season-long one. He brings a lot to the dressing-room and to the training pitch. Again, like Adrian, his personality is perfect for what we need in our group. He's a brilliant professional who does everything right and has the experience to contribute with advice when it's needed. Lonners is a top keeper as well, I'm buzzing he's with us.

Someone who is not a new addition, Caoimhin Kelleher, has kicked on again and is showing great signs of progression. He's clearly a big talent and we were all buzzing when he made his debut for us at MK Dons and pulled off some absolute worldie saves on the night.

He's lucky to have the likes of Ali, Ads and Lonners in and among him each and every session – as well as John Achterberg and Jack Robinson as coaches. But as with any pro having great people around you is one thing – you still have to be good enough and work hard enough. Caoimhin definitely ticks every box and you can see he's going to have a fantastic career.

Finally, it turns out we have a budding JK Rowling

in our ranks. James Milner's book is launched this week and in fairness it's absolutely brilliant. All joking aside, I know he's been asked for years to write an autobiography but, Milly being Milly, hates any fuss directed towards him personally. This format – 'Ask a Footballer' – is perfect for him.

Honestly – I'm not just saying it because he's a friend and team-mate – it's a superb book and I would strongly recommend buying a copy.

He'll not appreciate me saying this, because he hates compliments, but if there is a pro you can and should learn from stick Milly right at the top of that list. He's also very funny, in that dry Yorkshire way, so it's entertaining as well as informative.

You'll be glad to know he's made all the lads buy one, so you'll be in good company. I'd like to think I make the credits, as I submitted a couple of questions myself that made the final edit.

I'm pretty sure it's available to buy from tomorrow and I'm pretty sure he's doing a signing session in Liverpool. You'll need to check his social media to get full details – yep, the very same social media he said he'd never join. I don't need to explain why he broke that pledge in this column because he explains in the book.

Congrats anyway, Milly – it's a cracking read and the trainers and t-shirt are looking very fresh on the front-cover picture.

Liverpool 5, Arsenal 5 (after extra time, Liverpool win 5-4 on penalties)

Goals: Mustafi (6 og), Milner (43 pen), Oxlade-Chamberlain (58), Origi (62, 90)

Line-up (4-3-3): Kelleher, Williams, Gomez, Van den Berg, Milner (c), Oxlade-Chamberlain (Chirivella 81), Lallana, Keita (Jones 55), Elliott, Brewster, Origi. Subs not used: Adrian, Kane, Larouci, Clarkson, Koumetio

Caoimhin Kelleher was the hero for Liverpool in the shootout and had an evening he will never forget. He said: 'As soon as the final whistle went, all the focus was on trying to save in the shootout. Some of the lads and the coaches said to me, 'You've nothing to lose, just try to be the hero.' And luckily I did it in the end. It was a bit of a whirlwind. I'm obviously happy but it's just hard to sum it up at the moment. It's just unreal to be honest. We have a never-say-die attitude and we showed that once again, coming from behind on a few occasions. Div scored an unreal goal to keep us in it. It just goes right through the whole squad that we'll never give up. It was unbelievable tonight. Once you hear [the fans] singing You'll Never Walk Alone and you're actually playing, it's quite surreal. It's just an unreal feeling. It's class.'

Captain's contribution

Henderson was given the night off as Jürgen Klopp once more used Liverpool's brilliant younger players in the Carabao Cup.

NOV

2019

As the Reds' fine season continued apace, November brought another hectic month with wins across the board in the Premier League and Europe...

2nd: Aston Villa (PL) A
5th: KRC Genk (CL) H
10th: Manchester City (PL) H
23rd: Crystal Palace (PL) A
27th: SSC Napoli (CL) H
30th: Brighton (PL) H

Saturday, November 2nd, 3pm
Premier League
Aston Villa 1, Liverpool 2

Goals: Robertson (87), Mane (90+4)

*Line-up (4-3-3): Alisson, Alexander-Arnold, Lovren, Van Dijk,
Robertson, Lallana (Keita 84), Henderson (c), Wijnaldum (Oxlade-
Chamberlain 65), Salah (Origi 65), Firmino, Mane. Subs not used:
Adrian, Gomez, Fabinho, Milner*

*It was Sadio Mane's last-gasp strike that earned three points
for the Reds and continued their incredible form. He said: 'I'm
struggling to describe how happy we are but for sure we are
very happy and we deserved to win these three points, which
was really important for us. It's always going to be tough but I
think our reaction was perfect. In the first half it wasn't our best
performance but we just had to push hard as a team and give
everything and try, try again. That's what we tried to do and at
the end we created some chances and we scored two goals. We
deserved the three points.'*

Captain's contribution

A thrilling ending at Villa Park helped Liverpool leave
with three points. In a really tough game, Henderson was
solid, communicated well and constantly kept Villa's
midfield busy.

v KRC Genk
Tuesday, November 5th, 8pm

'COMEBACKS MAKE FOR GREAT TELEVISION BUT IT'S ON US TO ADDRESS THE ISSUE'

UEFA Champions League

THE gaffer's quote about this team being 'mentality monsters' is one everyone likes to jump on and after the weekend at Villa Park it was readily used again in both the mainstream and social media.

And it's right, of course. I think one of our biggest strengths as a squad and club at the moment is our ability to never give in and have total belief in what we are doing and that we can turn things around in any game or situation.

The numbers back up that 'Never Give Up' is more than just a slogan on a t-shirt for us – we've taken more points from losing positions than any other Premier League team in this moment. Of course that's a positive, but it's important we look at the other side of that stat as well.

Part of being 'mentality monsters' is that you challenge yourselves and always look at where you can be better.

As a team, do we like the fact that our mindset is 'keep going and never submit'? Yes, of course. But I would also like to think we'd look at those numbers and set ourselves the task of not putting ourselves in the position in the first place.

Comebacks make for great television, but it's on us as a squad to address the issue of falling behind in games. We want to be a side that dominates teams and takes total control of a game. We've proved time and time again we can do that, but clearly at the moment we haven't being doing enough to make sure we are in a dominant position on the scoreboard for longer periods.

There are many reasons you can find yourselves behind in a game and some of them are beyond your control. The opposition might be on fire and have a player who scores an absolute 'worldie'. You can also get bad luck, by which I mean a bounce of a ball or a poor decision.

But the truth is, the majority of the time a team goes behind is because they haven't done the right things in that moment. As a team we will look to address that.

To be clear, this isn't just about conceding. The issue is from front to back – every single department of the team – in terms of us not being ruthless enough in those moments. In some of the games we've gone behind in, we have probably not shown the intensity of play that characterises our best qualities. That's a team issue, the entire 11 selected to start.

Everyone knows and trusts that with this side it is never a case of a lack of commitment – that will never be an issue with this group. But it might be other issues that we are all guilty of, such as a slight dip in concentration, making the wrong decision or not taking enough care.

Regardless, if we really want to achieve the things that we all think we are capable of – as a team and club – we can't just rest on our laurels and take for granted that we'll always make the comeback.

There isn't a member of our squad who isn't determined to improve every single day. Part of improvement is being able to identify the correct areas to work on and find a way to address it. That's one of the most impressive things about this group of players: there is always a desire to improve and a desire to do better, even with the smallest of details.

It's nice to get the praise for the comebacks, but we'll be far more satisfied when we get to the point that the comeback isn't necessary.

Turning to tonight specifically, it's fantastic to be back at Anfield for another hugely important Champions League fixture and a local lad who has become synonymous with our European nights in the past two seasons is Jamie Webster.

Opposition fans might be sick of it but his performances of 'Allez Allez Allez' and other LFC songs became a big part of our fans' culture for the previous campaigns. There won't be a player in our team who hasn't seen the videos of Jamie performing at 'BOSS Nights,' on LFC tours and of course the fan-parks ahead of the two Champions League finals. The footage of him on stage in Madrid, before the game last season, is simply breathtaking.

Maybe the one drawback for Jamie, though, through his association with the club, is that people ignore the fact he's actually a top musician full-stop. He's not just someone who can belt out a great footie song. He's travelled with the team on tour a couple of times now and you'll not meet a nicer, more unassuming fella.

Jamie has released his first single recently and it's got nothing to do with football. It's called Weekend In Paradise.

As a team we wish Jamie all the very best with it and hope it's a big success. It's not that we don't want him performing the Liverpool songs anymore, but it would be magic to see a local lad, who has worked so hard, achieve his dream.

Liverpool 2, KRC Genk 1

Goals: Wijnaldum (14), Oxlade-Chamberlain (53)

Line-up (4-3-3): Alisson, Alexander-Arnold, Gomez, Van Dijk, Milner (c), Wijnaldum, Fabinho, Keita (Robertson 74), Salah, Oxlade-Chamberlain (Mane 75), Origi (Firmino 89). Subs not used: Adrian, Lovren, Lallana, Jones

Alex Oxlade-Chamberlain was named man of the match and after the game he said: 'I'm getting better with every game physically. It's nice to be chipping in with the odd goal. It all adds to your confidence.'

Captain's contribution

Henderson missed the game as Jürgen Klopp's side continued their Champions League campaign with a tight win against a committed KRC Genk outfit.

v **Manchester City**
Sunday, November 10th, 4.30pm

'IT'S IMPORTANT FOR A HEALTHY RIVALRY THAT YOU CAN RECOGNISE SOMEONE ELSE'S QUALITIES'

Premier League

IF I was to pick just one word to sum up how we as a squad feel about Manchester City, it would simply be: 'respect'.

Of course they are an opponent we've had decent tussles with over the past couple of seasons in particular, both domestically and in Europe, but as a team we have nothing but admiration for them.

What they've achieved as a team is something that everyone in sport, let alone just football, can look at and appreciate. They are relentless winners who have found the hunger to go again and again.

I think it's important for a healthy rivalry that you can recognise someone else's qualities and achievements without that leading to any sort of insecurity about what you're doing yourself.

As an example, I've never understood it when ourselves and City are asked whether we'd sooner win the Premier League or the Champions League, or then subsequently asked to compare which is more important or impressive.

I'd bet anything you like that you'd get the same answer in both dressing-rooms, whether there was a microphone in front of them or not: we want to win everything.

The other part of this is that ourselves and Manchester City aren't the only rivals this season when it comes to winning trophies domestically and I think it's daft to ignore the others who are just as competitive.

Chelsea are unbelievably impressive at the moment and I can see them pushing both of us all the way in the Premier League and having a massive say in the cups. We've played them twice already, in the league and the Super Cup, and they definitely have the players and the approach to go all the way.

Likewise Leicester City, who gave us such a tough contest at Anfield not that long ago. They still have players and staff who know from first-hand experience what it takes to do it and I haven't seen many weaknesses in their set-up to suggest they won't keep with the pace.

Anyone who thinks this is about just two teams is wrong and in our dressing-room we're certainly not foolish enough to get caught in that trap.

We have total belief in what we are doing and for occasions like today we always focus on our own qualities, like we do for every game we play regardless of the team we're facing.

But having a healthy amount of respect for the opponent, on and off the pitch, is important and I'm pretty sure both teams have that.

Away from today specifically, I'd like to use this column to encourage as many of our supporters as possible to come and watch our brilliant Women's team when they play Everton at Anfield a week today, Sunday 17 November.

It's the first time a Women's Super League match will ever be played here at our famous ground and is part of the FA Women's Football Weekend.

The Women's game is growing in this country and as the father of two daughters I know the success of the Lionesses in the World Cup during the summer, reaching the semi-finals, gave a big boost to participation and also viewing.

We've already seen some big occasions at other Premier League grounds for matches this season, with over 31,000 at the Etihad for the Manchester derby and 24,000 at Stamford Bridge for Chelsea v Spurs.

Plus I believe Wembley is sold-out for England v Germany on Saturday with a chance that the world-record crowd for the women's game might be broken.

A Merseyside derby is always a special occasion and it's no different for the Women's game, so I'd like to encourage Liverpool fans here today to come back in a week's time and show your support.

Liverpool FC Women can be inspired by the magic of Anfield in the same way we are, so I hope to see a really healthy crowd inside this great stadium giving them the backing they deserve.

Finally, on behalf of the entire team I would like to extend a warm welcome to Seán Cox and his family, who I am told is planning to attend the game today.

Seán's courage and that of his family is an inspiration to us all. Hopefully we can do him proud with our efforts today.

Liverpool 3, Manchester City 1

Goals: Fabinho (6), Salah (13), Mane (51)

Line-up (4-3-3): Alisson; Alexander-Arnold, Lovren, Van Dijk, Robertson; Henderson (c) (Milner 61), Fabinho, Wijnaldum; Salah (Gomez 87), Firmino (Oxlade-Chamberlain 79), Mane. Subs not used: Adrian, Keita, Lallana, Origi

Virgil van Dijk said: 'It's like any other three points of course but it was a bit special because you are playing against the champions, your direct rival, and I think it was a very good game to watch. We are very happy to get the three points. We all know – and we all feel – there are so many games left that so many things can happen between now and May. We are very happy with the position we are in, but we cannot take it for granted. They are the champions first of all, so they will definitely be up there again. The other teams have been doing well, too. The only thing we focus on is the game ahead of us, it's pretty boring and I keep saying it, but it is actually a fact. Let's just go for it.'

Captain's contribution

A passionate Anfield crowd roared Liverpool to victory and Henderson was in his element, offering calm leadership and a succession of superb passes, including a wonderful cross for Mane's goal that sealed the win.

Saturday, November 23rd, 3pm
Premier League
Crystal Palace 1, Liverpool 2

Goals: Mane (49), Firmino (85)

Line-up (4-3-3): Alisson, Alexander-Arnold, Lovren, Van Dijk, Robertson, Henderson (c) (Milner 79), Fabinho, Wijnaldum, Oxlade-Chamberlain (Origi 64), Firmino (Gomez 89), Mane. Subs not used: Adrian, Keita, Lallana, Salah

Trent Alexander-Arnold, alongside Virgil van Dijk, was rock-solid in Liverpool's defence and he was thrilled to leave London with the win. He said: 'It was a tough game and this is always one of the toughest places to come, Selhurst Park, with the crowd right on top of you it's going to be a really tough game. They've got some really good players and it's always, for some reason, really difficult coming here so we've done well to get the win. We knew it meant a lot so hopefully we'll be able to keep going and use this as momentum.'

Captain's contribution

Henderson rolled his sleeves up against a disciplined Palace side and his constant running and organising helped the Reds grind out a fine win on the road.

Jordan Henderson

v SSC Napoli
Wednesday, November 27th, 8pm

'OF COURSE, LUCK PLAYS A PART IN FOOTBALL; IT ALWAYS HAS DONE AND ALWAYS WILL'

UEFA Champions League

THERE'S a famous quote in golf that I think is credited to the legendary Gary Player, albeit Arnold Palmer can claim something similar, which says: "The harder you practise, the luckier you get..."

I've heard a lot in recent months about 'luck' playing a part in some of the wins we've managed this season. Of course, luck plays a part in football; it always has done and it always will.

But my experiences have shown me that the more you put into something, the more you get out – and that's the real story about our team at the moment.

My personal view is it is the professionalism of this squad and the dedication to what we are looking to achieve that delivers the so-called luck. Take the weekend's game as an example and our two goalscorers.

Sadio Mane spent the week with Senegal, including playing in Swaziland. Roberto Firmino was in Abu Dhabi with the Brazilian team.

Sadio took a pretty big knock in his game but came back to Melwood at the earliest opportunity and worked night and day to be fit and ready for selection against Palace.

His commitment to both club and country meant he wanted to give his very best for both and we saw at Selhurst Park, despite spending the previous two weeks almost constantly training or rehabbing, he was ready when it mattered. That's not luck – it's commitment to being the best he can be. Bobby bagged our winner late on and the way he kept going in the game is testimony to his belief in fighting for every inch. He, along with Fab and Ali, were playing in Abu Dhabi on the Tuesday, only reporting back for us quite late because of travel. But I didn't hear a single moan or excuse from any of those boys.

I've used Sadio and Bobby as examples but I could go on. Mo and Robbo were gutted to miss their games because of ankle knocks and in truth lesser pros wouldn't have been able to appear on our teamsheet at the weekend.

Again, their determination to contribute in whatever way possible means both made themselves available for the match. Trent and Ox also both played twice during the international break, as did Gini.

Only hard work and the highest standards allow the sort of moments we enjoyed in London on Saturday to happen. Without that, the so-called luck is completely irrelevant.

The other factor you need to have is bravery. You have to have courage in key moments.

I spoke in the week about how important mentality is in football, how it's just as crucial to a team as the collective and individual skills and ability of the players.

If you look around our dressing-room, we have a lot of leaders, a lot of big personalities and, overall, a group of great lads who have an incredible attitude towards the game, their work and how they live their lives outside of it. They all do everything they can to be at 100 per cent for the next game – and they do what they can to push their team-mates on alongside them.

We're entering a really busy period in our season now with so many games, so this is exactly the attitude we need within the dressing-room.

These lads make sure the standards don't drop, that they are set every single day and that's part of the reason why, I believe, we're able to produce results like the one on Saturday at Crystal Palace.

For the moment, we put the Premier League to one side as we concentrate on the Champions League and look forward to another European night at Anfield, something I know all of the lads absolutely relish.

Tonight we face Napoli and it reminds me that great things happen because both individuals and teams step up when the big moments come.

The games we've played against Napoli in the past year have been some of the toughest I've been involved in. Whether it be their ground or ours, it's always such a difficult contest.

They have world-class players and a world-class manager who is one of the game's great winners. They mix individual quality with collective organisation. Honestly, as a player, they are so, so hard to play against.

Last season the group was decided on Matchday Six in this very fixture. As it turned out, qualification to the next stage wasn't just decided during this game but essentially the very last kick of it.

Ali Becker's save, at a moment when there'd have been zero time for us to realistically get back in front, was one of those special moments. He didn't get lucky in that moment, he was able to call upon the hundreds and hundreds of hours of practice and training to react in the only way that was going to keep the ball out of the back of the net. Crucially, he showed huge courage in decision-making.

We are still very much in the early stages of the season in my view and as always our concentration is on the only thing that matters in this moment: the next game. But it's an encouraging sign that, as a team, we have the ability to show our best when it really matters.

Liverpool 1, SSC Napoli 1

Goal: Lovren (65)

Line-up (4-3-3): Alisson, Gomez (Oxlade-Chamberlain 57), Lovren, Van Dijk, Robertson, Henderson (c), Fabinho (Wijnaldum 19), Milner (Alexander-Arnold 78), Salah, Firmino, Mane. Subs not used: Adrian, Lallana, Shaqiri, Origi

Jordan's post-match reaction: 'We would have liked to have won tonight to finish the job off, but Napoli are a good side and made it difficult and we could only get a point. They're a good team with good players so we knew it would be difficult. There were times where obviously we could do better but there were times where we played some good stuff. In the second half we were just searching for the second one, we couldn't manage to get it but we keep going. Like I say, we're still in a healthy position but we need to get a result away now. We'll stay positive. We've still got a job to do away but we're confident we can do that.'

Captain's contribution

On a night where Liverpool struggled to impose their authority on the game, Henderson's work-rate and desire stood out. His high energy approach came to the fore, as did his spell at right-back during the second half when he showed his usual willingness to do everything required to try and help Liverpool win.

Jordan Henderson

'AS CAPTAIN, I'M A FIRM BELIEVER IN SETTING THE HIGHEST STANDARDS'

Premier League

ONE of the things that we take great pride in as a team is our ability to defend as a team. It's not about individuals and it's not solely about the defence, it's about every single one of us doing our jobs when we haven't got the ball.

That was a key factor in the success we enjoyed last season and we continue to set ourselves the highest standards when it comes to defending collectively but, unfortunately, we're in a bit of a run in which clean-sheets are proving harder to come by.

It's not that we're conceding a particular type of goal. If we were, it would be easy to identify the issue and to fix it in training. It's a mixture of instances in different situations and for whatever reason they're not going in our favour – but whatever the cause we have to put it right.

It can be a midfielder winning a tackle, a forward closing down, a group of us pressing at the right moment, a defender getting a bit more support at particular moments; basically about finding that little bit extra in all areas and before we know it we'll be matching the standards that we set ourselves.

Why am I so confident? Simple: we've done it before so we can do it again. This group has proven itself on so many fronts over the last few years but sometimes you get little reminders to step up and I've no doubt that we will respond in the right way.

We know it's an area for improvement and whether we win, lose or draw, we always look at what we could have done better. Why? So we can improve as best we can.

The good thing is this isn't a bad situation; it's anything but. We've got ourselves into a really strong position through some brilliant results but, like any top side, we're constantly on the lookout for any tweaks that will bring improvement, individually, collectively or both.

That we're doing this from a position of strength speaks volumes for the desire and professionalism of this squad. We want to be as hard to beat as possible and we want to get back to keeping clean sheets.

What I would say, though, is that our main obsession is to win games and if we keep on doing that even the harshest self-critic among us won't be too disappointed by the odd goal going against us.

As captain I'm a firm believer in setting the highest standards and that's even more important at a club like Liverpool where we want to be going for the biggest prizes and taking responsibility for absolutely everything.

Again, I'm blessed in this respect because when I look around the dressing-room I see a group of players who are driven to be the best that they can be for the good of themselves and the club.

That will be the case today when we face a Brighton team which is showing a lot of promise under Graham

Potter and we know they will come to Anfield looking to take our scalp.

It's up to us to face that threat down and the stronger we can be without the ball, the better the chance we'll have of being effective when we're in possession.

There was a lot of talk in midweek after the draw with Napoli about our position in the Champions League and prospects of qualifying for the last 16. I can assure everyone reading this that we've put all thoughts of Europe to one side for the time being and we're fully focused, firstly, on the challenge we face today.

We also have crucial matches with Everton and Bournemouth to come before we even begin to think about Salzburg and qualification for the next stage of the Champions League.

We spoke about what we could have done better against Napoli, and the things we did well, immediately after the game. Then after that, all of our focus has been on today's game.

We're back at home and we want three points and if we're to do that, we'll need the backing of the supporters once again.

The lads commented after the game how the atmosphere in the second half on Wednesday helped us as we were looking to get the equaliser against Napoli and it's always an advantage for us when we're at home.

That support will be crucial once more if we're to get

another win against a tough Premier League opponent under our belts today.

Liverpool 2, Brighton 1

Goals: Van Dijk (18, 24)

Line-up (4-3-3): Alisson, Alexander-Arnold, Lovren, Van Dijk, Robertson, Oxlade-Chamberlain (Adrian 78), Henderson (c), Wijnaldum, Salah (Lallana 69), Firmino (Origi 76), Mane. Subs not used: Milner, Keita, Gomez, Shaqiri

Virgil van Dijk scored a brace for the Reds and was in his usual imperious form at Anfield. He said: 'We're disappointed with the way we ended the game. We conceded a bit of a strange free-kick, the red card for Alisson. But it's not easy to play every couple of days and make sure we are more than 100 per cent. The beginning of the first half was good, towards the end of the first half I think we should have done better. It was not an easy game. We had to dig deep and we did. With my height and my ability to be dangerous in the box, I could be even more effective. But it's not easy to always be marked by the best defensive header of the opponent. But today I was able to sneak away twice.'

Captain's contribution

Henderson led from the front against a Brighton side that offered plenty of threat. Playing in a more central role, Henderson tackled well, passed with intelligence and was a real leader during a game that stretched the Reds to the maximum.

DEC

2019

The busiest month of the season brought a whole new set of challenges for Henderson including a Merseyside derby, Champions League clashes and a bid to be crowned world champions...

4th: Everton (PL) H
7th: Bournemouth (PL) A
10th: RB Salzburg (CL) A
14th: Watford (PL) H
17th: Aston Villa (CC) A
18th: CF Monterrey (CWC) N
21st: Flamengo (CWC) N
26th: Leicester City (PL) A
29th: Wolverhampton W (PL) H

Jordan Henderson

v Everton
Wednesday, December 4th, 8.15pm

'IT WAS A SHOW OF SOLIDARITY, LOVE AND DEFIANCE WHICH SHOWED THIS CLUB AT ITS BEST'

Premier League

THIS evening both Everton and ourselves will be supporting the Rainbow Laces campaign, which has become an increasingly important one in football over past seasons.

For those who are not aware, it is something devised by Stonewall and looks to show support for members of the LGBT community, some of whom still find football an environment that isn't as inclusive as it should be.

Along with representatives of other Premier League clubs, I was asked last week about the impact on supporters in particular and it did make me think. I've been blessed in my life not to have been subjected to discrimination personally, but I was in Bulgaria with the England team recently when the racist abuse aimed at a number of our team was absolutely despicable.

The idea that in this country, in this day and age, members of the LGBT community don't feel like they can attend football matches and be who they are, without fear of being subjected to abuse, is heartbreaking.

The campaign is also aimed at players – at all levels of football, professional and amateur – to send the message that sexuality is not a barrier to enjoying being part of this amazing game.

I know there is often a discussion about the lack of openly gay players in the English professional game for men, but from my perspective I know in our dressing-room it wouldn't be an issue, let alone a problem.

As we've seen with other areas of discrimination it's actions that really matter, but I think campaigns such as this are important to set an agenda. It's not really about the laces themselves, the campaign has become bigger than that – it's about the positive message of inclusivity to members of the LGBT community.

At Liverpool, because not all the players have boots that require laces, we choose to show our solidarity through the captain's armband and the manager wearing the laces to symbolise the whole team supporting it.

I do think it's an area where we can all do more to understand the hurtful impact that homophobia has on those wanting to play or enjoy watching football, so hopefully the awareness raised around these next few games will help with that.

Tonight's game obviously needs little introduction as we welcome Everton to Anfield for the Merseyside derby.

I was told I have played against Everton 13 times as a Red and, therefore, I know from experience what to expect tonight: derbies are just different. But like any other game, we go into this one mainly focusing on ourselves and what we can do to affect the game.

We're fully aware of the threat and quality of Everton's players and we know we'll need a big performance if we're to get what we want from it.

There's obviously been a lot of talk once again, after

the results at the weekend, about our position at the top of the table, but take it from me – no-one within this squad of players or coaches has given it a thought. We're only concerned with tonight's game against Everton.

Finally I want to take this opportunity to pay tribute to the Hillsborough families, those who survived the tragedy and everyone who has played a part in the 30-year campaign for justice.

Last Thursday's verdict was yet another of those occasions when, as a player, you are left humbled by their integrity and perseverance in the face of adversity. I know I speak for the dressing-room and the club as a whole when I say all involved continue to have our full support and it will always be this way.

That message was delivered magnificently by the supporters during the first six minutes of Saturday's game against Brighton. I have been fortunate to play in some wonderful atmospheres at Anfield but this was special in its own right because it was a display of solidarity, love and defiance which showed this club and this city at its unique best.

I cannot speak on behalf of Everton, but given the way they have supported this cause for the last three decades I have no doubt that they share our feelings.

Tonight we will be divided, and that's the way football rivalry should be, but the way they have stood shoulder-to-shoulder with us when it mattered most is something that does Everton Football Club enormous credit.

Liverpool 5, Everton 2

Goals: Origi (6, 31), Shaqiri (17), Mane (45), Wijnaldum (90)

Line-up (4-3-3): Adrian, Alexander-Arnold (Gomez 83), Lovren, Van Dijk, Robertson, Lallana (Henderson 72), Wijnaldum, Milner (c), Shaqiri, Origi (Firmino 73), Mane. Subs not used: Kelleher, Keita, Oxlade-Chamberlain, Salah

Double goal hero Divock Origi enjoyed another eventful derby. He said: 'It's a special atmosphere, a special game. I think as a team we just enjoy it. There were a lot of goals today and we showed that we really enjoyed to play for Liverpool. The manager showed us trust and we just tried to repay it as much as possible and get the three points. We know it's important for our season. It's an important game, it's special, you can hear it. I'm so happy. I think the first was important just to break the game open. The second one, I enjoyed that. It was a great pass from Sadio for the first and [then] a wonderful ball from Dejan. We used the space well, that's one of our weapons, going in behind. It was wonderful service and that was good today.'

Captain's contribution

Henderson started the game on the bench but was brought into the contest towards the end in a bid to consolidate an important result. A lovely long pass set up a chance for Mane but the forward couldn't convert.

Saturday, December 7th, 3pm
Premier League
Bournemouth 0, Liverpool 3

Goals: Oxlade-Chamberlain (35), Keita (44), Salah (54)

Line-up (4-3-3): Alisson, Gomez, Lovren (Alexander-Arnold 40), Van Dijk, Robertson (Jones 76), Milner, Keita, Henderson (c), Oxlade-Chamberlain (Shaqiri 87), Firmino, Salah. Subs not used: Adrian, Elliott, Mane, Origi

Jordan's post-match reaction: 'It was a professional performance and a very solid performance. Overall, we are delighted with that. Offensively, I thought we were very good, we kept the ball for large periods of the game and we defended really well as well, so overall we are really pleased.'

Captain's contribution

Henderson helped the Reds move 11 points clear at the top of the Premier League and he was brilliant throughout, producing some sublime passes to keep Liverpool on the front foot. His diagonal ball created Alex Oxlade-Chamberlain's opener and encapsulated Henderson's afternoon, and his talent.

Tuesday, December 10th, 5.55pm
UEFA Champions League,
RB Salzburg 0, Liverpool 2

Goals: Keita (57), Salah (58)

Line-up (4-3-3): Alisson, Alexander-Arnold, Lovren (Gomez 53), Van Dijk, Robertson, Keita (Origi 87), Henderson (c), Wijnaldum; Mane, Firmino (Milner 75), Salah. Subs not used: Adrian, Jones, Shaqiri, Oxlade-Chamberlain

Virgil van Dijk said: 'We had to be ready – and ready for a very tough night because they are a good side. They play a little bit similar to what we try to do, direct and try to get in behind the defence and stretch them. We had to be ready and we dealt with it and then obviously at the end of the first half we had the opportunities to score for 1-0, maybe 2-0 but unfortunately we didn't do that. The belief is always there but you have to show how much you really want it. The goals we scored were very good, the whole second half I think everyone looked comfortable.'

Captain's contribution

Henderson displayed his usual leadership and tenacity in a fine performance in the middle of the pitch. His tackling, running and passing game were all of the highest calibre as Liverpool booked their spot in the Champions League knockout stages.

v Watford
Saturday, December 14th, 12.30pm

'WE'RE BLESSED WITH AN INCREDIBLY TALENTED AND DETERMINED SQUAD'

Premier League

WE'RE back at Anfield today as the games keep coming thick and fast for us in all competitions.

A lot of us are asked in interviews how we find such a schedule as players and the demands it places upon us. And yes, it is tough – very tough. But we're very lucky at Melwood to have the best people around us to keep us in the best shape possible before, during and after games.

From our fitness and sports-science teams, our medical staff and the guys who work with Mona and the kitchen staff on nutrition and supplying us with the right things to eat and drink, everyone pulls together to give the lads the best possible chance of being at their maximum come matchday.

It really is a team effort at Melwood, and across the club, as I have stated in these notes on many occasions before. We, as players, are incredibly grateful for everyone's hard work and dedication.

We're also blessed with an incredibly talented, hungry and determined squad, all eager to contribute to helping us achieve our collective goals.

One of the things I keep hearing is how we would cope if we picked up a few injuries. It's a question that I can't quite get my head around because, like every team, we've had our fair share of knocks already.

The key thing is that when one of us does have to drop out for whatever reason, whoever comes into the team is making light of whatever absences we have. That is credit to everyone involved. Obviously it is credit to the players themselves for having the right mindset and to the manager for utilising the squad in a way which has allowed us to pick up some great results in recent weeks.

But this credit also has to be extended to the staff behind the scenes: the physios, the masseurs, the medical department and everyone else who plays a role in preparing us. I know, as players, we get the headlines when things are going well, but I can safely say I'm speaking for all the lads when I say that the support we get from everyone at Melwood should be highlighted every bit as much as whatever we do on the pitch.

Their work is always vitally important, that goes without saying. But at this stage of the season – when the games are coming thick and fast and it's inevitable that we'll all get the odd ache and strain – it is absolutely invaluable, none more so than when we're playing away in Europe in midweek and then have an early kick-off on Saturday.

That is the challenge that we're facing today, but it is one that we will meet head on against a Watford side that needs the points as much as we do.

We faced a really tough game in Salzburg in midweek against a very energetic, lively and dangerous side, but ultimately I felt we demonstrated just how far we've developed as a team by the manner in which we seized control of it. It won't come as any surprise if we were to hear of Salzburg getting big results against Europe's top sides in the future, but I think Virg [van Dijk] highlighting the maturity in our performance afterwards was spot-on.

In fact, on another night we could have won the game far more comfortably, but we did the job – and Mo decided if he was going to take one chance all night, it was going to be the toughest one of them all. I've no idea how he scored from where he did, but that's why he is one of the very best in the business.

All over the park there were big performances and we needed them to get the job done. We can now look forward to Monday's draw, but we'll be putting thoughts of the Champions League to one side until next year.

It was a similar story at Bournemouth last weekend when we produced another controlled display against a very good side to get the three points and keep our first clean sheet in a while, which we were all delighted with.

Of course, you'll all remember our last Anfield game very well 10 days ago. It was one of the best Merseyside derby performances since I came to the club.

In each of these last three games, we've had players stepping in and making huge impacts: Divock against Everton got a lot of headlines, of course; Naby has two goals in two starts; Ox and Shaq have both also been on the scoresheet and put in brilliant performances, too.

It underlines my earlier point about needing everyone in the squad being ready to come into the team and produce what we know they're capable of. It really is credit and testament to them and they've deserved the praise they've received.

Come kick-off today, we'll have been as well prepared as possible by the staff, and once the whistle goes, it'll be up to those 11 players on the pitch to produce against a side who will be every bit as determined as we are.

Enjoy the game.

Liverpool 2, Watford 0

Goals: Salah (38, 90)

Line-up (4-2-3-1): Alisson, Alexander-Arnold, Gomez, Van Dijk, Milner, Henderson (c), Wijnaldum (Robertson 59), Shaqiri (Oxlade-Chamberlain 70), Firmino (Origi 88), Mane, Salah. Subs not used: Adrian, Keita, Lallana, Williams

Jordan's post-match reaction: 'They've got a new manager and we knew they'd make it very difficult for us. We'll take the three points and move on. [The second goal] took a while because of VAR again! But we were delighted to wrap it up at the end.'

Captain's contribution

Henderson had to dig deep during a testing game at Anfield where the Reds never hit top gear. It was a quiet game from the skipper but his effort, as always, ensured the Reds' fans respected his afternoon's work.

Tuesday, December 17th, 7.45pm
Carabao Cup quarter-final
Aston Villa 5, Liverpool 0

Line-up (4-3-3): Kelleher; Hoever (Norris 82), Van den Berg, Boyes,
Gallacher, Kane, Chirivella, Christie-Davies (Clarkson 77), Elliott,
Longstaff (Bearne 65), Hill. Subs not used: Winterbottom, Clayton,
Dixon-Bonner, Stewart

Neil Critchley's post-match reaction: 'We had some information
at half-time from the manager – basically to keep playing the
way we were playing, keep being brave, keep doing what we were
doing. So he was out there watching with the staff and the players
and I hope, and I'm sure he will be, he is proud of the way we
played tonight.'

Captain's contribution

Henderson was with the rest of Liverpool's more
recognised first XI outfit in Qatar for the FIFA Club
World Cup but watched this game from afar alongside
the rest of the Reds overseas.

Wednesday, December 18th, 5.30pm
FIFA Club World Cup semi-final
Monterrey 1, Liverpool 2
Khalifa International Stadium

Goals: Keita (12), Firmino (90)

Line-up (4-3-3): Alisson, Milner (Alexander-Arnold 74), Gomez, Henderson, Robertson, Lallana, Keita, Oxlade-Chamberlain, Shaqiri (Mane 68), Salah, Origi (Firmino 85). Subs not used: Adrian, Lonergan, Jones, Williams

Jordan's post-match reaction: 'The most important thing was the win [and] we defended pretty well for the majority of the game. We would have liked to have scored another couple of goals, but overall I think we've got to be delighted. I felt we did control the game. We didn't create too much. We had a couple of half-decent chances but thankfully we managed to get one right at the end.'

Captain's contribution

Henderson's willingness to do whatever it takes for Liverpool to win was brilliantly illustrated by his efforts against Monterrey. Jürgen Klopp asked him to play at centre-back due to illness and injury to the likes of Virgil van Dijk, Dejan Lovren, Joel Matip and Fabinho and Henderson stood up to the new challenge.

Saturday, December 21st, 5.30pm
FIFA Club World Cup final
Liverpool 1, Flamengo 0 (after extra time)
Khalifa International Stadium

Goal: Firmino (99)

Line-up (4-3-3): Alisson, Alexander-Arnold, Gomez, Van Dijk, Robertson, Henderson, Keita (Milner 100), Oxlade-Chamberlain (Lallana 75), Mane, Salah (Shaqiri 119), Firmino (Origi 105). Subs not used: Adrian, Lonergan, Wijnaldum, Jones, Hoever, Elliott, Van den Berg, Williams

Jordan's post-match reaction: 'I'm delighted that we've come here and done what we wanted to do and that's win. We've had two tough games with extra-time but I thought the lads kept going and showed a great mentality again to find the winner. From the summer we've kicked on again. We've kept going and we've used it to help us progress and used it to stay hungry. So we need to do the same with this one.'

Captain's contribution

Liverpool became world champions for the first time in the club's history thanks to Roberto Firmino's extra-time goal and Henderson again cut a delighted figure as he lifted the trophy afterwards.

Thursday, December 26th, 8pm
Premier League
Leicester City 0, Liverpool 4

Goals: Firmino (31,74), Milner (pen 71), Alexander-Arnold (78)

Line-up (4-3-3): Alisson, Alexander-Arnold, Gomez, Robertson, Van Dijk, Wijnaldum, Henderson (Lallana, 82), Keita (Milner, 70), Mane, Salah (Origi, 70), Firmino. Subs not used: Adrian, Williams, Shaqiri, Jones

Trent Alexander-Arnold scored the Reds' fourth goal and said: 'I don't get on the scoresheet too often. [It was] a good counter-attack, I saw the space and Sadio has played a lovely ball and I thought, 'Hit it first time'. It was good to get the goal but the three points are what we came here for and we're made up to have them. You don't think you're going to be 13 points ahead but we're happy to be in this position, we're not going to take it for granted and we know the season is not over.'

Captain's contribution

Henderson received a standing ovation from the travelling Liverpool fans when he was substituted towards the end, and rightly so. He helped the Reds boss this game to send a signal to the whole of the division that Liverpool mean business and his organisational ability and will to win were huge assets.

v Wolverhampton Wanderers
Sunday, December 29th, 4.30pm

'THE LAST THING I EVER WANTED WAS TO BE JUDGED DIFFERENTLY BECAUSE OF MY AGE'

Premier League

I HONESTLY can't think of a more surreal experience in my career than being sat in Doha, with the Liverpool team and management, watching another Liverpool side play a competitive game.

I know a lot has been said and written about the rights and wrongs of the schedule and the decisions made that led to this situation. But I hope what wasn't lost was the commitment and bravery of our team that featured that night in Birmingham.

It was 10.45pm local time in Qatar when the match at Villa Park kicked off. Obviously it was the night before our semi-final in the FIFA Club World Cup and, under normal circumstances, players would have their routine and most would be in bed.

A mixture of the time difference meaning we hadn't adjusted our sleeping patterns at that stage of the trip (three hours ahead of UK time), plus a determination to support the team the best we could, meant all of us stayed up to watch.

The word that best summed up the performance was 'courageous'. And I don't mean that in a patronising way at all. I played first-team football as a teenager and the last thing I ever wanted then was to be judged differently to the senior players purely because of my age.

But you cannot ignore the average age of that team was, according to our esteemed club statistician, 19 years and 183 days old. The youngest-ever Liverpool side to compete in a competitive fixture.

So I think the bravery of the approach to the game is significant and worthy of mention. We all saw the opening stages of that game. Liverpool on the front foot. Aggressive in approach. Looking to be positive and take the game to Villa. It was a proper 'go on boys' moment.

However, I think the real mark of the courage shown was not to alter that approach even when they fell behind. It would have been easy and excusable to freeze and go into their shells – but they didn't. They stuck to their principles and our way of playing. It was brilliant.

We had Caoimhin, Sepp, Ki-Jana and Harvey join us in Doha the next day and each and every one of us was quick to congratulate them on their attitude and performance.

Again, even saying this now I worry it appears condescending, but it isn't. There won't be a player in our senior squad who hasn't gone through a tough experience on a football pitch. It's what you take from that experience that defines its impact. That's why we were proud and quick to say 'well done'.

I thought the whole situation reflected the quality of leadership at our Academy in Kirkby, if I'm being honest. Neil Critchley and the staff who took the game at Villa should be unbelievably proud of themselves.

They did Alex Inglethorpe and the club in general a great service in how they conducted themselves on and off the pitch.

Any organisation is only as good as the people who lead it and it's clear our Academy has outstanding leaders throughout.

I saw what Critch said in the build-up about it being a wonderful learning opportunity for the players and he was right. He set the tone with how he spoke about the chance for these young players to experience something special as a team.

The result wasn't special, admittedly, but the approach and performance was excellent – as was the humility shown at full-time. It was an 'opportunity' and they all made the best of it.

The other people to emerge with massive credit were the travelling LFC supporters at Villa Park that night. It was notable watching on the TV in the team hotel that the singing from the away section was non-stop. Honestly, you could hear it for the entire 90 minutes – there wasn't a player or staff member with us in Qatar who didn't comment on it.

That was an unbelievable show of class and more importantly a demonstration of understanding of the situation we and they were in.

It would have been easy to give that game a miss. It would have been easy to go and watch without getting behind the team, because the task looked so thankless. And – particularly at this time of year – it would have been easy to get off early, given the result.

The boys who came from Villa Park to Doha all said the support from the stands meant the world to them and it speaks volumes about the togetherness at the club that our fans stayed with them.

So, losing was tough to take and there is an overriding feeling of frustration that the schedule meant our progress in the Carabao Cup was directly affected by us trying to win the FIFA Club World Cup. The two groups impacted most by this were the players and the supporters.

It's on others to find a solution so this doesn't recur for Liverpool or any English club in the future, but as a first-team squad here, we were very proud of the team who represented us in the League Cup quarter-final and just as proud of the fans who went.

Hopefully it's an experience, that no matter how valuable for the younger players, doesn't have to be repeated in the future. But if it does happen, we know we have a group of young lads and coaching staff leading them who'll take the right approach and represent our club in the best way.

Liverpool 1, Wolves 0

Goal: Mane (42)

Line-up (4-2-3-1): Alisson, Alexander-Arnold, Gomez, Van Dijk, Robertson, Henderson (c), Wijnaldum (Milner 86), Lallana (Keita 67), Firmino (Origi 86), Mane, Salah. Subs not used: Adrian, Jones, Elliott, Williams

Adam Lallana impressed at Anfield and believes everybody in the Liverpool set-up is going to have to play a part in their success this season. He said: 'It's a squad game and I've said before that we're going to need everybody. We've got a few injuries at the time being and three or four kids on the bench, it's a great experience for them being involved and so close to what's been a special season so far. We can't take our foot off the gas. We've got a couple of huge games at home in the next week – Sheffield United, who have had a fantastic season, and then the derby in the cup. A couple of big games that we can see in the next week. We want to maintain that form going into the New Year and keep Anfield a fortress.'

Captain's contribution

This was Henderson's 308th Premier League match of the decade, more than any other player – he beat fellow Liverpool midfielder James Milner by one game! – and he was a strong, authoritative presence for the Reds in a match where patience was the key to victory.

JAN

2020

The new year saw Henderson more determined than ever to help Liverpool continue to win games and win trophies...

2nd: Sheffield United (PL) H
5th: Everton (FA) H
11th: Tottenham (PL) A
19th: Manchester United (PL) H
23rd: Wolverhampton W (PL) A
26th: Shrewsbury Town (FA) A
29th: West Ham (PL) A

Jordan Henderson

**v Sheffield United
Thursday, January 2nd, 8pm**

'WE WILL NOT CHANGE OUR APPROACH AT ANY POINT DURING THIS CAMPAIGN'

Premier League

AS the manager has said many times over, one of the great strengths of this team is that we don't allow ourselves to get comfortable, complacent or distracted at any point.

The nature of what we do and how it's covered these days means there is a lot of 'noise' to block out. But only being focused on 'what's next' instead of 'what might be' is a big characteristic in our dressing-room.

And if there was ever any danger of allowing in thoughts that might dim that focus, you only have to take a quick glance at the fixture list for January to realise the hard work has only just started.

Starting today, against one of the toughest teams we've faced so far this season, we have six matches to play in the first month of the new year. Depending on results, there could yet be a seventh or even an eighth game.

Obviously we are only interested in Sheffield United at the moment. It's the most important game of the season because it's the next one. But looking at the quality of teams we have to play this month is sobering. I actually see it as a good thing.

The Wolves game was one of the hardest I can remember for a very long time. We had to fight and scrap for every inch.

I can tell you now, today will be just as difficult, if not more so, against another opponent who plays positive football, with a work-rate that means you barely get a chance to breathe when on the ball.

When you're playing opponents who you know are going to push you to the limit you have to raise your own game. We've done that so far, but if we ease back even half a per cent we'll pay the price.

That's the Premier League in a nutshell. You come through one challenge and the next one is there waiting for you. It's unrelenting and unforgiving. If you think about the finish line before you've made it over every hurdle you'll 100 per cent end up falling flat on your face and allow the rest to overtake and get there first.

So that's where we are at. The next hurdle is Sheffield United tonight and we have to give everything we have to clear it.

A crucial part of this mentality is making sure, individually and collectively, we set ourselves the highest of standards and look to maintain or even better them.

Inside the dressing-room we have a lot of good leaders, a lot of big characters, who every day are pushing each other on to make sure the level doesn't drop in training, that we're pushing ourselves to improve even further.

We look to do that in every single training session, to make sure it's at 100 per cent.

It wasn't that long ago there was a lot of focus on our lack of clean sheets. I can tell you now that mattered to all of us, not just the defenders. Our expectation of ourselves was to do better in that area and we have seen an improvement. But we don't feel content about it – we want more.

Set a standard, meet it, then look to exceed it. Never stop focusing on what we can do better. That's our mantra.

An individual who has embodied that recently for us has been Joe Gomez. The start to his season wasn't straightforward. He had setbacks to contend with and challenges to face.

We all know what a massive talent Joe is, but at this level it's also about perseverance. It's meant the world to all of us to see how he's stepped up yet again and is playing with such confidence and control.

Joe isn't someone who is bothered about individual praise and he'll be the first to say that, in terms of contribution to the team, he has even more to give. But I think his situation is a great example to any player that hard work and only hard work is the path to achieving something special – be it as a person or a team.

Regardless of all the external talk around us at this moment, I can promise Liverpool supporters that we won't change our approach at any point during this campaign.

Until the very last kick of the very last game our only objective is to be better in the next match than we were in the one before it.

It's been an attitude that's served us well until now and there is no chance we're going to change it.

Liverpool 2, Sheffield United 0

Goals: Salah (4), Mane (64)

Line-up (4-3-3): Alisson, Alexander-Arnold, Gomez, Van Dijk, Robertson (Lallana 88), Milner, Henderson (c), Wijnaldum, Salah (Elliott 90), Firmino, Mane (Origi 78). Subs not used: Adrian, Phillips, Jones, Williams

James Milner was drafted into the starting XI late on following an injury to Naby Keita in the warm-up and, as always, the veteran midfielder gave his all for the Reds. He said: 'I didn't find out [I was playing] until we went into the dressing room after the warm-up. But the boys are always prepared, we're ready to go. We always do the right things so it's not a problem for anyone to step in. If you're mentally switched on anyway, I don't think it's too much of a big deal. If you just feel you're a sub, you're not ready – but I don't think anyone has got that mentality here. I'm pretty sure all of the lads would be able to do it. It was a good team performance, some good goals in there and we could have had a couple more.'

Captain's contribution

Liverpool were simply too good for Chris Wilder's side and Henderson had a fine game, ensuring the Blades' midfield had a torrid afternoon at Anfield.

v Everton
Sunday, January 5th, 4.01pm

'I'M SURE MICK WILL HAVE HIS COLLECTION BUCKET OUT AT ANFIELD THIS AFTERNOON'

FA Cup third round

I THINK I can safely say that one of the most remarkable sights over the Christmas period has been of a bloke walking around in nothing but his swimwear.

For most at today's game Speedo Mick will need no introduction, but for anyone who isn't aware of who he is and what he does then his name is definitely worth a quick Google.

I first heard about Mick a couple of years ago, but I don't think I have the words to do him justice. People who are actually from Liverpool tell me he's become a local hero because of the work he does for charity and, given what he's up to at the moment, it's easy to see why.

Mick's latest escapade is a walk from John O'Groats to Land's End wearing nothing but his trademark Everton swimming trunks and a Santa hat as he looks to raise £100,000 for community projects for local young people.

His efforts thus far have attracted a lot of media attention and rightly so, because it's bad enough going out without a coat at this time of year, never mind anything else.

I'm reliably informed that Mick is planning on taking a break from his charity walk so he can be at today's game and if he does make it I hope he gets all the support that he deserves.

I know he'll be wanting an Everton victory and I'd be the last to wish for that to happen, but it would be great if the two sets of fans could come together as they have so many times in the past to get behind Mick.

The rivalry between the two clubs in a footballing sense is obviously a fierce one, and rightly so. Who doesn't love a derby? But I have to say, ever since I was lucky enough to come to this city, it's always impressed me how the fans can put that rivalry to one side to come together in solidarity for good causes.

I really think it's something the city of Liverpool should be immensely proud of.

I'm sure Mick will have his collection bucket out at Anfield this afternoon so hopefully it will be filled and maybe next time we see him he might actually have his clothes on!

Liverpool 1, Everton 0

Goal: Jones (71)

Line-up (4-3-3): Adrian, Williams, Phillips, Gomez, Milner (c) (Larouci 9), Lallana, Chirivella, Jones, Elliott (Brewster 79), Minamino (Oxlade-Chamberlain 70), Origi. Subs not used: Kelleher, Mane, Henderson, Hoever

Curtis Jones hit a wonder-strike with 19 minutes left to help Liverpool to victory and he was delighted afterwards, especially as he is a local lad and a lifelong Reds fan. He said: 'The gaffer's strong on not showing when you're hurt and showing when things are tough so I think it was only right that I didn't show that I was ill [before the game]. I'm glad I didn't because

I went out there and I put in a shift for the team. I'm just happy that we came away with the win and I'm looking forward to the next round.'

Captain's contribution

Henderson was rested for this encounter as Liverpool manager Jürgen Klopp entrusted the club's youngsters with a derby encounter. He was amply rewarded as they comfortably beat Everton to claim Merseyside bragging rights thanks to a sublime goal from youngster Curtis Jones, who sealed his place in Merseyside derby folklore.

Saturday, January 11th, 5.30pm
Premier League
Tottenham 0, Liverpool 1

Goals: Firmino (37)

Line-up (4-3-3): Alisson, Alexander-Arnold, Robertson, Van Dijk, Gomez, Henderson (c), Wijnaldum, Oxlade-Chamberlain (Lallana, 61), Firmino, Salah (Shaqiri 89), Mane (Origi 81).
Subs not used: Adrian, Minamino, Phillips, Williams

Gini Wijnaldum had an impressive game alongside Henderson in midfielder and had particular praise for matchwinner Roberto Firmino. He said: 'Every day when we are training or playing a game, we try to do it better than we did before. We always strive to do it better. Bobby is really important for the team – not only with the goals but also with the way he plays. He works a lot, assists a lot and because of the way he plays, the team can play better. He is important in all parts.'

Captain's contribution

Spurs away from home is always a testing challenge and this match was no different. Henderson did well to break up the home side's possession and was constantly looking to get forward when he could. It was a solid display during a victory that took Liverpool 16 points clear at the top of the Premier League table.

Jordan Henderson

v Manchester United
Sunday, January 19th, 4.30pm

'A ONE PER CENT DIFFERENCE IN THIS LEAGUE IS ENOUGH TO BE PUNISHED'

Premier League

LIVERPOOL versus Manchester United is the sort of fixture that, if you weren't directly involved in it like we are, you'd still make sure you planned your day around being able to watch.

There hasn't been a period in my lifetime, regardless of how either club was doing at the time, where this wasn't one of the standout games of the season.

It's the sort of match that captures the imagination of football supporters up and down the country, regardless of club loyalty, because it's such a big rivalry.

As Liverpool players we're often asked where does this game rank compared with the Merseyside derby? Do we see it as bigger or more important? I don't know for certain, but I'd imagine it's the same for Man Utd with the Manchester derby.

The answer is easy really. It's as big and it's as important, but it's different.

As a professional I've been taught to respect every opponent. As a Liverpool player you know you have to respect the importance of this match in particular and a big part of that is recognising the strength of United as a club and as a team.

I've never liked the idea of any other club being a benchmark for us. We should never define ourselves by what others have done. For me, Liverpool's benchmark is Liverpool. We don't need anyone else's achievements to drive us on.

I want to be successful for Liverpool because of what it means to our fans. Not because it means we can claim we've outdone someone else, no matter how big the rivalry.

One of this team's biggest strengths is that we set our own standards and our own expectations. We don't need external motivation – it's within us.

The only outcome we ever look ahead to is trying to win the next game. The only situation we care about being 'the best' in is the match we're playing in.

When the gaffer says we don't talk about records in our dressing-room he's spot-on. No one here is interested in anything other than winning the next match – simple as. Why? Because, in the here-and-now, records are not important. The time for reflection will come later.

We manage to keep this tunnel-vision because we have great respect for every team we face and that's never been more relevant than when we play Manchester United.

I've lost count of the amount of games we've gone into with people drawing conclusions before the team bus has pulled up at the ground, let alone the game itself has started. The second we let any of that outside noise impact us, we won't perform to the levels needed to maintain or exceed what we're currently doing.

United are a world-class team with unreal players. I've played with a number of them for England. They're as good as anything out there.

To name just two games, we've seen away at Chelsea in the Carabao Cup, and at Manchester City in the Premier League, what they are capable of. If we don't focus entirely on putting all we have into getting the best result we can today, we'll get punished.

Our mentality was very clear at Spurs away. I know some people thought our reaction at full-time was odd because it wasn't celebratory, but why would it be? Were we pleased to win? Yes! But we were exhausted because of how hard the game was. We also knew the next major test and hurdle was only a few days down the track.

The Tottenham game demonstrated in 90 minutes how hard it is to be successful in the league. For so much of the game we were great and in control. But the moment we dropped, even a tiny bit, the momentum changed.

We have to stay alert to this and on our guard. It doesn't matter what the situation looks like, it can change if you lose your focus.

A one per cent difference in this league is enough to be punished, so that's why having players who understand just how vital each second of every game is, is so valuable.

I can't think of a better example of that from last week than Adam Lallana. He proved, with his performance and impact, that playing at your maximum all the time isn't just helpful – it's critical.

He showed a mentality at Spurs that we all need to embrace in these coming games, starting today. By that I mean treat each tackle, header, pass, shot, block or save like it's the most important moment of the season. The importance of winning individual battles accumulates to winning the collective one. Adam embodies that and his performance in London was a textbook demonstration of it.

I'm sure today's game will be hyped up all over the place and, as I said at the beginning, if I wasn't involved directly I'd be one of those getting caught up in it. But as players it's different.

For us, and the United squad, it's just about winning the game – the extra significance and context doesn't come into it. Winning today is all the motivation we need and hopefully we can do the job.

Liverpool 2, Manchester United 0

Goals: Van Dijk (14), Salah (90)

Line-up (4-3-3): Alisson, Alexander-Arnold, Gomez, Van Dijk, Robertson, Oxlade-Chamberlain (Lallana 65), Henderson (c), Wijnaldum, Salah, Firmino (Origi 82), Mane (Fabinho 82). Subs not used: Adrian, Minamino, Matip, Jones

Jordan's post-match reaction: 'We're not really thinking about the end. Why should we change now? Why think about the end of the season? There are still a lot of games left; we have taken it each game [at a time] for a long time now and it has put us in good stead. So there is no need to change. The crowd were unbelievable again today. For us as players, it's the next game, the next challenge – the Premier League is tough, there are some tough teams. United played well at times today but, overall, I felt we deserved the three points.'

Captain's contribution

Henderson was at his energetic, bustling best against United and drove the Reds to victory with a wonderful performance. He was unlucky not to score in the second half when his effort rattled the post and a goal would have been a nice way to cap off what was one of Henderson's best performances of the season.

Thursday, January 23rd, 8pm
Premier League
Wolverhampton Wanderers 1, Liverpool 2

Goals: Henderson (8), Firmino (84)

Line-up (4-3-3): Alisson, Alexander-Arnold, Robertson, Gomez, Van Dijk, Henderson (c), Oxlade-Chamberlain (Fabinho 70), Wijnaldum, Salah (Origi 85), Firmino, Mane (Minamino 33). Subs not used: Adrian, Williams, Jones, Matip

Jordan's post-match reaction: 'You know it's going to be difficult here as we've seen over the season. They're a good team, they make you work. We knew it'd be difficult but we knew to keep going, keep fighting. We defended really well, the big man and the back four were brilliant again. We had some chances as well to put the game to bed, which I keep saying over the last couple of weeks, so that's something that we want to improve on and kill the game off earlier. But [we] showed the mentality again to keep going and finding that winning goal.'

Captain's contribution

Henderson's superb form continued at Molineux as he headed the Reds in front early on before setting up Roberto Firmino towards the end to confirm the three points. It was another authoritative, passionate performance from the Liverpool skipper.

Sunday, January 26, 5pm
FA Cup fourth round
Shrewsbury Town 2, Liverpool 2

Goals: Jones (15), Love (og 46)

Line-up (4-3-3): Adrian, Williams, Matip (Salah 79), Lovren, Larouci, Fabinho, Chirivella, Jones, Minamino (Firmino 85), Elliott (Oxlade-Chamberlain 71), Origi. Subs not used: Kelleher, Keita, Hoever, Alexander-Arnold

Adrian was selected in goal for the Reds and praised Shrewsbury's efforts after the contest. He said: 'They deserve all the respect we give them. We respect all the rivals obviously but when we are on the pitch it's 11 against 11, so you give everything for the result. At the end, they got a draw and obviously it's like a win for them because we have to play the second game now at Anfield.'

Captain's contribution

Henderson was rested for this tie as the Reds struggled to overcome a Shrewsbury Town side who were desperate for a win or, failing that, a replay at Anfield.

Wednesday, January 29th, 7.45pm
Premier League
West Ham United 0, Liverpool 2

Goals: Salah (35 pen), Oxlade-Chamberlain (52)

Line-up (4-3-3): Alisson, Alexander-Arnold (Keita 77), Gomez, Van Dijk, Robertson, Henderson (c), Wijnaldum, Oxlade-Chamberlain (Jones 85), Origi (Fabinho 69), Salah, Firmino. Subs not used: Adrian, Lovren, Minamino, Matip

Alex Oxlade-Chamberlain looked sharp and scored Liverpool's second. He said: 'There are a lot of tough games coming up so we've just got to keep plodding along and keep doing what we are doing to first and foremost achieve what we want to do in the league. We want to keep that going and if records come off the back of that then that's obviously a little bonus.'

Captain's contribution

Henderson filled in at right-back during the second half, again emphasising his versatility and his amazing team-first approach. Another hugely impressive showing from the Reds' skipper, who has been in the form of his life of late.

FEB

2020

A brilliant January had seen
Liverpool go unbeaten with six wins
and a draw. Could Henderson and the
Reds keep that form up as the season
raced towards a fascinating conclusion?

1st: Southampton (PL) H
4th: Shrewsbury Town (FA) H
15th: Norwich City (PL) A
18th: Atletico Madrid (CL) A
24th: West Ham United (PL) H
29th: Watford (PL) A

Jordan Henderson

'I HOPE DANNY HAS A STINKER TODAY, BUT I KNOW IT'S HIGHLY UNLIKELY'

Premier League

WHAT can I say about Danny Ings? Well, firstly I hope he has a stinker today, but I know it's highly unlikely.

When Southampton came to Anfield last season Danny wasn't eligible to play because his first season at St Mary's was a loan. It's different this time around, now the move is officially permanent. It means today we all have to cope with trying to stop one of the most dangerous centre-forwards in the Premier League.

To say those of us who shared a dressing-room with him here at Liverpool are buzzing to see how he's doing this season is an understatement.

Ingzi was so popular with everyone at Melwood. He's one of those people who'd brighten up any room with his positivity. Incredibly funny, always warm, never short of a smile.

Everyone knows his story with us and how a couple of major setbacks played a part in robbing us of more minutes of Ingzi on the pitch. But those setbacks didn't diminish his contribution overall.

How he conducted himself, the attitude he showed, his desire and his professionalism was genuinely inspiring. It made an impact on a lot of us and still does. But focusing on personality and character does a massive disservice to his greatest asset – his ability.

Ingzi was only ever a nice guy off the pitch. On the pitch he was 'horrible' in the best sense of the word from a footballing perspective: wouldn't give you a second to breathe on the ball, always snapping away to try and win the ball back, constantly offering and always a threat.

I go back to what I said right at the beginning and I hope after the match today I'm telling him "hard luck." But we'll also be telling him that we're all made up to see him doing what he does best.

The fact he's getting the recognition he deserves as one of the best centre-forwards, in one of Europe's best leagues, is reward for all the hard work he's put in for a very, very long time.

Moving back to our current squad, Curtis Jones has had a lot of nice things said and written about him in the last few weeks and rightly so.

When he has had a chance to play in the first team he has shown the kind of ability that we see on a daily basis at Melwood, and he's even managed to score a couple of really good, important goals that have helped the team a lot.

That's the kind of impact that any young player wants to make, but it can only happen if their attitude, application and approach is absolutely spot-on.

It isn't just about what you do on the pitch either. What you do off it is every bit as important, whether that relates to the food you eat, the people you have around you, or the way you conduct yourself. It all counts.

That's why it was great to see Curtis visiting a local children's charity called KIND last week.

It wasn't so long after his goal against Everton which made him a bit of a local hero – at least for the red half of the city – so to see him among a load of kids was really positive, especially as they were all from a similar background to himself.

People often talk about footballers 'giving back' to their communities, but I don't see it like that and I know the lads all feel the same way. We are part of our community and, like everyone else, we want to be involved whenever and wherever we can.

Sometimes it will be seen and sometimes it will be unseen, but the basic aim is always the same: to be part of things and to make a difference whenever possible.

In Curtis' case, that meant going back to KIND, a brilliant charity where he'd spent time as a schoolboy, and I know that he will have got as much out of the visit as the kids did, if not more.

When you see that kind of work up close you can't help but feel comforted in the knowledge that we are blessed to have some brilliant people in this city who are doing wonderful work that benefits the whole of society.

There are no guarantees in football, but I am sure that Curtis will be better for this experience and as captain I was proud to see him getting involved with such a good cause that means a lot to him.

In its own way, this was just as important as his derby goal because it will stand him in such good stead going forward.

Liverpool 4, Southampton 0

Goals: Oxlade-Chamberlain (47), Henderson (60), Salah (72, 90)

Line-up (4-3-3): Alisson, Alexander-Arnold, Gomez, Van Dijk, Robertson, Henderson (c) (Lallana 88), Fabinho, Wijnaldum (Minamino 81), Salah, Firmino, Oxlade-Chamberlain (Keita 73). Subs not used: Adrian, Lovren, Matip, Origi

Jordan's post-match reaction: 'I'm enjoying this season, we've put in some really good performances. Everybody is enjoying their football but it's also about the work ethic and giving everything for each other – and that's the most important thing to me. Just give everything you can for your teammates, which we have been doing. It's always nice to get a goal, especially at Anfield. But the most important thing was the three points. We're getting closer to our target but I don't see why we need to change – I keep saying it every week but it's the truth. We take the next game as it comes, that's the next challenge and the biggest challenge.'

Captain's contribution

Henderson continued his fine form as he completely ran the show for Liverpool, scoring the Reds' second goal and giving Southampton's midfield no room for manoeuvre. It was a brilliant showing from the captain.

Tuesday, February 4th, 7.45pm
FA Cup fourth round replay
Liverpool 1, Shrewsbury Town 0

Goal: Williams (og75)

Line-up (4-3-3): Kelleher, Williams, Hoever, Van den Berg, Lewis, Chirivella, Clarkson (Dixon-Bonner 89), Cain, Elliott (Boyes 89), Jones, Millar (Hardy 82). Subs not used: Jaros, Gallacher, Bearne, Norris

Curtis Jones produced a fine showing and and he was delighted to help Liverpool progress to the FA Cup fifth round. He said: 'The boys, the coaches, the staff that have trained all week have been absolutely unbelievable and it's a proud moment for me to be the youngest player to captain the Reds. I'm happy that we topped it off with a win for our great fans. It's a dream come true.'

Captain's contribution

Henderson, alongside the rest of Liverpool's recognised first XI squad, were rested for this match by Jürgen Klopp.

Jordan Henderson

Saturday, February 15th, 5.30pm
Premier League
Norwich City 0, Liverpool 1

Goal: Mane (78)

Line-up (4-3-3): Alisson, Alexander-Arnold, Gomez, Van Dijk, Robertson, Wijnaldum (Fabinho 60), Henderson, Keita (Milner 84), Oxlade-Chamberlain (Mane 60), Salah, Firmino.
Subs not used: Adrian, Lovren, Lallana, Origi

Jordan's post-match reaction: 'We are just delighted to get the three points, it's good that Sadio is back after his injury and he's straight on the scoresheet, so nice to have him back and nice to get the three points. It was pretty hard-fought. We had to go right until the end, of course, but that's Premier League football. Norwich City are a good team and have caused teams a lot of problems throughout the season and got some good players, so we knew it would be difficult. It was difficult conditions for both teams in the end but, overall, I think we've got to be delighted with the three points.'

Captain's contribution

Henderson provided his fifth assist of the season, setting Mane up for the game's most crucial moment and the Liverpool captain was energetic and positive throughout this difficult encounter.

Tuesday, February 18th, 8pm
UEFA Champions League round of 16
Atletico Madrid 1, Liverpool 0

Line-up (4-3-3): Alisson, Alexander-Arnold, Gomez, Van Dijk,
Robertson, Fabinho, Henderson (c) (Milner 80), Wijnaldum,
Mane (Origi 45), Salah (Oxlade-Chamberlain 72), Firmino.
Subs not used: Adrian, Keita, Minamino, Matip

Joe Gomez said of the first-leg defeat: 'It's disappointing and
not something we're used to. But if anything, it just gives us
that motivation to bounce back and make it right as quickly as
possible. Sometimes it happens and you need to take the positives
from it. It gives us that hunger again – not that we didn't have it
but we just want to bounce back and make it right. That's what
we'll try to do.'

Captain's contribution

Henderson provided his typical energy and commitment
but Liverpool could not get the result they were hoping
for. A hamstring issue meant Henderson also had to be
replaced by James Milner towards the end.

Jordan Henderson

v West Ham United
Monday, February 24th, 8pm

'NO ONE HATES LOSING MORE THAN THIS SQUAD, I CAN TELL YOU'

Premier League

136

ONE of the best qualities of our squad in recent seasons has been the ability to respond positively to setbacks. It's probably a misconception this season that we haven't experienced many. I can tell you we have – all the time in fact.

We've had setbacks and adversity within games and we've reacted in the right way. We've had setbacks and adversity with injuries and illness and we've reacted in the right way. We haven't lost that many games as a club recently, but when those defeats have come we've reacted in the right way.

I think the reason for that is quite simple: we don't make anything bigger than it needs to be. We view every setback as a problem that has a solution. As a group our culture is: find that solution.

Losing in Madrid was disappointing, bitterly disappointing. But perspective is important and so is not over-inflating it. Truth is, the tie is only at half-time, so there's a long way to go.

As the manager said, we always remain calm at half-time during a 90-minute game and look at how we can positively impact the second half, so why wouldn't we do that when we have three weeks to prepare for the return? And we'll have Anfield behind us that night, too.

But the other truth is that we need to draw a line immediately as that return leg isn't until next month and we have lots of work and challenges before then. Our mantra has been, for a long time: focus on the next game and only the next game. That's what we'll do.

And, by the way, it's not hard to refocus because the task ahead of us tonight is really tough. West Ham are a team packed with international quality players, with a manager who is vastly experienced in getting positive results, and with a desire and hunger to improve their situation.

If our focus is anywhere other than entirely on trying our best to win this game we'll suffer another setback without doubt.

The words spoken by Virgil van Dijk and Andy Robertson after the game in midweek sum up where our heads are at as a dressing-room. Both made the point that we immediately switch focus to the Premier League and West Ham United coming to Anfield.

It's very much a mentality of 'work to do'. And it's the right mentality. Whatever the noise around us, whatever the topic being discussed, we have to concentrate on what we can affect.

This is a massive game for us. The only thing we can affect is what the outcome of this game is. We can affect that by making sure we come into this game with the right amount of humility and ambition and stay true to the values that have brought us this far.

No one hates losing more than this squad, I can tell

you, but we have built into our team culture an ability to respond in a positive way to setbacks – whatever form they take.

We're going to need to dig deep into that in the coming days, weeks and months because the challenges are only going to get greater and the hurdles higher. To be honest, we wouldn't want it any other way. And we're ready for it.

Speaking of challenges, a number of the lads have asked me to reference the support we got away at Norwich and Madrid in this programme. It won't have escaped anyone's notice that the weather in England in the past few weeks has meant travel for day-to-day life has been difficult. West Ham experienced it themselves with their match away at Man City having to be rescheduled at late notice.

Getting to and from Norwich was far from straightforward for us as a team and we have the luxury of having all our needs catered for us, and some of the best people in the business sorting our travel.

The away ends at Norwich and Madrid were full and the backing we got was so loud and supportive. It wasn't lost on us players that a lot of those in the away end probably had no guarantees on knowing how their journeys home would be affected.

It's moments like this when you realise how privileged we are to have the following we do. People travelling at all times, by different means, at great expense – and it's never straightforward. It's very humbling when you stop and think the reason they do it is to support our team.

And it's not just Liverpool fans – it's football fans in general. People who travel hundreds of miles, taking time off work and having to get up early and arrive home late.

There'll be no trains after the game tonight for the thousands from London coming to cheer on our visitors. I'm sure there'll be lane closures on motorways as well.

It doesn't take a series of storms to bring home the sacrifices fans make for their teams. But after Norwich, in particular, and around the Madrid game, it did highlight that no matter how challenging it is for players in these periods, it's a tiny fraction of the issues supporters deal with.

So, on behalf of the Liverpool players, we massively appreciate it and we never take it for granted.

Liverpool 3, West Ham United 2

Goals: Wijnaldum (9), Salah (68), Mane (81)

Line-up (4-3-3): Alisson, Alexander-Arnold, Gomez, Van Dijk (c), Robertson, Keita (Oxlade-Chamberlain 57), Fabinho, Wijnaldum, Salah, Firmino, Mane (Matip 90). Subs not used: Adrian, Lovren, Minamino, Lallana, Origi

Gini Wijnaldum got the Reds up and running against West

Ham with the opening goal and was pleased to help Liverpool win. He said: 'We just want to continue this run we're in right now. We know what we have to do, we don't want to leave it with this, we just want to carry on and try to keep the good momentum. We work really hard for it and hopefully we can keep it until the end of the season. If you go back a few years ago, we made mistakes. But we learned from the mistakes we made and I think that's why we are so good right now – we have a team that has played with each other for a few years. During the years we learned a lot and that's why we are so good right now.'

Captain's contribution

Henderson's hamstring injury prevented him from taking part in this contest and while Liverpool undoubtedly missed their captain, the Reds managed to squeeze past a committed West Ham United team at Anfield.

Saturday, February 29th, 5.30pm
Premier League
Watford 3, Liverpool 0

Line-up (4-3-3): Alisson, Alexander-Arnold, Lovren, Van Dijk, Robertson, Fabinho, Wijnaldum (Lallana 61), Oxlade-Chamberlain (Origi 65), Mane, Salah, Firmino (Minamino 79). Subs not used: Adrian, Matip, Jones, Hoever

Andy Robertson accepted that Liverpool were beaten by the better side on the day and was hoping for a quick reaction. He said: 'It's up to us to now bounce back because today wasn't good enough, simple as that. Watford deserved the three points, they were brilliant to a man. And we weren't. It's up to us to now show that this defeat hurts and up to us to now go and put a run together that will crown us champions.'

Captain's contribution

Henderson was again absent as the Reds' amazing Premier League run came to an end at Vicarage Road on a day when Liverpool never really got going.

MAR

2020

As Liverpool inched their way towards
the Premier League title, March saw
the season interrupted in the most
unusual, and tragic, way imaginable...

3rd: Chelsea (FA) A
7th: Bournemouth (PL) H
11th: Atletico Madrid (CL) H

Tuesday, March 3rd, 7.45pm
FA Cup fifth round
Chelsea 2, Liverpool 0

Line-up (4-3-3): Adrian, Williams, Van Dijk, Gomez, Robertson,
Fabinho, Lallana (Salah 80), Jones (Milner 70), Minamino, Mane,
Origi (Firmino 70). Subs not used: Lonergan, Oxlade-Chamberlain,
Matip, Chirivella

Adam Lallana was one of Liverpool's brighter performers and
was disappointed to see the Reds exit the FA Cup. He said:
'There were big moments in the first half where we failed to
score. A couple of mistakes and if you let a good team like
Chelsea counter on you like that, they're going to have chances.
We're bitterly disappointed with the result. Credit to Chelsea.'

Captain's contribution

Henderson missed this contest as Liverpool were well
beaten at Stamford Bridge.

v Bournemouth
Saturday, March 7th, 12.30pm

'THE MOST CRUCIAL THING OF ALL IS THAT WE CONTINUE TO SHOW FAITH IN EACH OTHER'

Premier League

A LOT of people have had their say about our form in recent weeks and we have to accept that, especially seeing as we've had a lot of plaudits this season, both as individuals and as a team.

We also have to shut it out, though, otherwise we would just end up being caught up in the speculation at a time when we need to keep our focus and our sense of perspective.

That's no different to when we've received praise either, by the way. Throughout the season we've collectively blocked any acclaim out and focused on our jobs at hand.

And the reality is no one needs to tell us that we haven't played well enough lately. We're a team that's built on honesty and self-awareness and that means we know better than anyone else when we have to do better.

That's where we're at right now and the sooner that we can get back to the standards that we've set ourselves the better. But part of that process is remembering our qualities and not being distracted by the noise outside.

The reason why we are in such a strong position in the Premier League is because it is what our performances since the start of the season have deserved. Again, we can't ignore that fact. Just as we can't get too carried away when we're winning, nor can we get too despondent when results aren't going our way.

The simple fact is we are the same team. We have the

same players, the same management, the same staff and the same supporters. We have shown consistently that we can deal with challenges and this is just another one that we have to face.

The good thing is none of us got carried away when there was talk of being invincible and winning this trophy or that trophy. Again, that talk came from outside rather than from ourselves. We just concentrated on going from one game to the next, treating the opposition with respect and doing our very best. This approach has served us incredibly well so why would we change?

Luckily, if there's one thing this group has shown it's how to respond to adversity. We have seen that on so many occasions so it's only a matter of time – and hard work – before we see it again. The most crucial thing of all is that we continue to show faith in each other.

I know the supporters won't have enjoyed the last few weeks as much as the ones that came before it and we want to put things right for them as well. But for that to happen we will need the backing of the fans because they can make such a massive difference. Hopefully we can feed off one another.

We have two home games now, starting today, and we'll be doing all we can to get back on track – and those in the stands can also play their part, as they continually have done.

Aside from the games, there have been a couple of

significant departures from our set-up recently and on behalf of the team I want to use this column as a chance to say a big thank you for their contribution.

Our doctor, Andrew Massey, one of our physios, Richie Partridge, and the U23s coach, Neil Critchley, have all chosen new and exciting challenges.

Doctor Massey and Richie were popular, trusted and respected figures at Melwood. The relationship between players and medical staff is always a close one – it's the nature of what they do. As a dressing-room we're pleased they've left on great terms. Both are welcome back any time they wish and will remain part of the LFC family because of their contribution.

Critch is a little different, because being based at Kirkby means some of us had limited contact with him. That said, the younger players who are now part of the first-team set-up speak about him in amazing terms and when he was in and around the first team set-up he was always impressive.

We're very grateful for how he's helped shape a number of the young pros in our dressing-room and also for the manner in which he led the team twice this season in difficult circumstances against Aston Villa and Shrewsbury Town.

I'm sure he won't need it, but we wish Critch all the luck in the world at Blackpool and hope he makes a success of a great opportunity.

As Alex Inglethorpe, the Academy director said, it shows there is a pathway to progression and improvement at Kirkby for coaches as well as players – and that's going to serve the club well in the future.

Liverpool 2, Bournemouth 1

Goals: Salah (24), Mane (33)

Line-up (4-3-3): Adrian, Alexander-Arnold, Gomez, Van Dijk, Milner (c), Oxlade-Chamberlain (Lallana 84), Fabinho, Wijnaldum, Salah, Firmino (Origi 90), Mane. Subs not used: Lonergan, Keita, Minamino, Matip, Williams

Mo Salah scored Liverpool's first which meant he had netted 70 goals in his first 100 Premier League appearances for the club – seven more than the next best. The brilliant Egyptian was just thrilled to help the Reds earn another important win. He said: 'I always love to score and help the team to get the points and today we showed our personality after [going] 1-0 down, so we had to react to that and I think we did well and we got the result. We need to keep going for the next three games and the rest of the season.'

Captain's contribution

Henderson's injury issues continued as Liverpool returned to winning ways against Eddie Howe's side. The win put Liverpool an astonishing 25 points clear at the top of the Premier League.

Jordan Henderson

v Atletico Madrid
Wednesday, March 11th, 8pm

'THE WORST SEAT IN THE GROUND WHEN I'M NOT INVOLVED IS THE ONE NEXT TO ME'

UEFA Champions League round of 16

LIKE any other player, I hate missing games. While we all accept injuries as an occupational hazard, we would give anything to avoid them, which is why we spend so much time with the physios and masseurs who do everything they possibly can to keep us fit.

I think I have said before in this column that I'm far away from the 'perfect' patient during these moments. In fact, impatience and frustration are things I struggle to hide. But when injuries do happen you just have to deal with them as best you can and take positives wherever you can find them.

I'm a terrible 'watcher'. By this I mean the worst seat in the ground when I'm not involved is the one next to me. You can ask Andy Robertson after Saturday's game against Bournemouth.

But there was one element of 'watching' at the weekend that was enjoyable and it was being able to properly take in the importance of Anfield. I got a lot of pleasure from being able to take more notice of the Kop on Saturday than would usually be the case and it's no exaggeration to say that it looked absolutely incredible.

Before the game it was immense. And for a 12.30 kick-off it was even more impressive. I know kick-off time shouldn't really matter to atmosphere, but we all know it does. I think it's a situation where players and supporters share similar feelings.

As a player you have to gear yourself up mentally for a match that kicks off at that time because it isn't 'the norm'. It is the little things like eating chicken and pasta at 9.30 in the morning that are hard to compute.

For fans it's the fact that if you're travelling to the game you have to be up earlier and you've had less time for the tension and excitement to build.

None of these are excuses though and the early kick-offs have been around long enough now that we have all found ways of managing ourselves through them.

Going back to my earlier point, one of the biggest differences between playing and watching is that, as a player, you can 'zone out' from certain things at certain times.

Every player is different of course, but personally speaking in those final moments before the match starts I try and get in a tunnel-vision mindset. The only thing I want to concentrate on is visualising the first tackle, header or pass. There is one exception to that, though, and that's taking a few seconds to take in what's happening on the Kop.

Being a supporter on Saturday, I made a point of properly soaking in the feeling around Anfield in those final few minutes and seconds and in particular what was happening on the Kop. It made me realise why it's so important.

It was genuinely incredible to look at with all the colours and flags and the noise was unreal. It looked and sounded amazing.

I know I've mentioned Spion Kop 1906 in these notes previously, but the work they do and the effort they put in is always worth highlighting because it makes such a positive impact. They, more than anyone, are responsible for making the feeling so raw and authentic.

I saw on social media that they had 50 new flags made for the Bournemouth game and, from a player's point of view, the Kop looked better than ever. I don't know if you've noticed, but if you watch our players just before we assemble for kick-off, most have a proper look at the Kop and try to take a moment to take it all in.

Part of having something special in life is making sure you never take it for granted. That counts for so many things – but as a Liverpool player the positive impact of Anfield and the Kop should be top of that list.

I know going into tonight's game there'll be a lot of talk about the importance of us being at home. There will no doubt have been dozens of articles and broadcasts referencing historic and special Anfield European nights, but we can never and will never take it for granted.

It never 'just' happens. These occasions come because we make it happen – all of us.

People from groups like Spion Kop 1906 bring the

colour – the supporters bring the passion – and then as players we have to bring the intensity of performance. The moment we assume things will happen for us just because it's Liverpool and it's Anfield and it's the European Cup, then it won't.

None of us take any of this for granted and we come into this game knowing if we want something special to happen, we have to work hard to make it so.

That's what we'll look to do as players: give everything we have and, if we do, we know the support will be there driving us on.

Liverpool 2, Atletico Madrid 3
(Atletico Madrid win 4-2 on aggregate)

Goals: Wijnaldum (43), Firmino (94)

Line-up (4-3-3): Adrian, Alexander-Arnold, Gomez, Van Dijk (c), Robertson, Oxlade-Chamberlain (Milner 82), Henderson (Fabinho 105), Wijnaldum (Origi 105), Salah, Firmino (Minamino 113), Mane. Subs not used: Lonergan, Lallana, Matip

Jordan's post-match reaction: 'Obviously we're really disappointed. I thought the performance overall was very good, the intensity and everything we spoke about before the game. We put everything into the game and we're bitterly disappointed. We'll be disappointed with the goals we've conceded, but if we look at the performance then large parts of the game we'll be pleased with – but we're just obviously disappointed with the goals we've conceded. With the position we were in and to

*concede the goals we did isn't like us, so it's very disappointing
but we've got to take it on the chin. We just couldn't find the
net, we couldn't find that third goal to kill the game off. We left
everything on the field and that's what is important. It's hard to
play against a team that defends very well and that is how they
play. But we created a lot of chances, it's not like we didn't create
them. Overall we're so disappointed and for the rest of today and
tomorrow it won't feel nice, but we have to use it to help us finish
the season strong. Our focus is now on the derby, that's up next.
It's a big game, and we'll just take it game by game to ensure we
can finish this season strongly.'*

Captain's contribution

Henderson returned to the Reds' line-up for a big
night of European action under the Anfield lights and
helped his side take the tie by the scruff of the neck.
Liverpool harried and harassed their opponents – with
their skipper at the heart of everything –and wrestled
the initiative in the tie only for Atletico to snatch it in
extra-time.

Following the Atletico Madrid match, growing concerns about the Coronavirus pandemic led to the indefinite postponement of the remainder of the football season. Liverpool's hopes of winning the Premier League title were, rightly, delayed for the time being as the world united to try and combat the problem.

During a worrying time for everyone, Henderson spoke about the challenges ahead.

'FOOTBALL ISN'T
EVEN IN OUR
THOUGHTS
AT THE
MOMENT. YOU
UNDERSTAND
THAT THERE
ARE BIGGER
PROBLEMS IN
THE WORLD'

It's a slightly unusual way for us to do this interview, but it's quite an unusual time for everybody all across the world at the moment. How challenging has this been for you – not just as a footballer but as a dad and a husband?

Yeah, it has been different, it has been challenging at times, especially when you've got three kids running around the house! But at the same time I feel as though I'm in a luxury position if you like, in terms of I've got a garden, a nice house that the kids can go and run around and play in, go in the garden and play. I understand a lot of people might not have that luxury. I'm surrounded, obviously, by my wife and kids, so it makes it a lot easier. But there's people out there who are a lot worse off who are suffering more than I am and my thoughts really just go out to them. It sort of puts everything into perspective a little bit.

The footballer's psyche is always about if you suffer a defeat, it's all about the next game. But that's been the perspective that we've all had, whatever job we're doing at the moment, that there are bigger things and bigger forces at play at the moment...

Football isn't even in our thoughts at the minute. Of course myself and other players will be wanting to get back as soon as possible and be chomping at the bit to go and play football. But at the same time, you understand that there's bigger problems and bigger things going on in the world. We just need to do our best to support our families, stay safe and just keep listening to what the authorities are telling us. And hopefully this period can finish sooner rather than later and everybody can start some normality off again sooner rather than later.

What has this period been like for you as a footballer?

It's a totally different test. My biggest downs in my career up until this point were obviously injury, I would say. That was the hardest thing for me to deal with personally, but this is a different challenge. The time that I've spent with my family and my kids over the last couple of weeks is something that I've never been able to do before, so I'm just trying to take a lot of the positive things around it. I've really enjoyed being with the kids every day, helping them with their school work and things that I wouldn't normally do. I've just tried to do it as much as I can and enjoy it. But when it is 24/7 it can be challenging at times as everybody will know! But I've just tried to enjoy this period that we're going to get. I know it will be for a long period, of course, but just stay positive and try to enjoy it as much as I can because I've never really had a block of time like this to be with the kids and my wife for a long time.

Have you got newfound respect for teachers and the job they do each day? What are you like as a dad that's home-schooling at the moment?

I have been helping them with that. To be honest, I've enjoyed doing that. That's something I've never really done apart from the homework when they're coming home from school and you're helping them with that. But to do it every day in the morning and help them with certain things, I've quite enjoyed that. Like I said, you don't get opportunities to do that often, so I'm trying to make the most of it.

The squad is a very close-knit unit and you'll be having to use WhatsApp groups and that kind of thing. How active are those at the moment?

We've got a big WhatsApp group and things are getting fired in quite often, so everybody's sort of staying in contact and chucking different videos in and different challenges that we can do. There has been a lot of contact with the lads because normally we're spending every day together and travelling together and all sorts of stuff. To not see each other for a long period of time is strange, especially at this time of the season. But at the same time, when we have the off-season, again, it's pretty similar to that. It's just the time that we're at and the stage that we're at in the season that it is a little bit different. Now we're in the house and you can't really do anything else, it is a bit strange.

Are you mindful that you have to stay in touch with some of the younger players to keep their spirits up in what is a very challenging time?

I think it is important to stay in touch with people, especially the lads. Some people cope differently to others. Some of the lads are on their own who I've spoken to, which must be really difficult. Most of the lads have family and kids and stuff, which will make it easier – maybe a little bit more difficult at times! But overall a lot easier when you've got family around you and people around you. But when you're on your own it must be so difficult, so I've touched base with those lads and they seem okay but it's only been a couple of weeks and we've probably got a few more months to go at least.

It's made everybody united in the world with the challenge that's going on. We've seen the great human side come out with things like foodbank donations. You know about this group of lads and how this will bring the best out of them as human beings...

Definitely. It's an important time for everybody to come together – not just our club but everybody in the country and in the world. It's important that everybody comes together and we try to just listen to the advice that we've been given to make sure that this virus sort of goes away sooner rather than later and everybody can get back to some sort of normality soon. It's a time to come together and help each other. I'm sure there's other ways of doing that, especially supporting the NHS and the work that they're doing – you can see how much support they're getting from the whole country, so that's really important as well. But for us as players, [I'm] thinking of different things that we can do all the time. I'm sure the lads will help, which we have already with the foodbanks, but if there's anything else then I'm sure the lads will be on board to do so.

Do you have a message for the fans? They're aware of what's going on in the world, but they're really missing their team...

We're missing them too, that's for sure! I would just say stay safe, of course, stay inside and keep listening to all the advice that the government and the authorities have given us. If we do that, this will sort of pass quicker than we hope. But just try to stay positive. It's a perfect sort of chance to use our song that we sing every game in terms of You'll Never Walk Alone – it's the perfect opportunity for that. I've seen stuff on social media where the nurses were singing along to it, but stuff like that is really powerful. This is the time where it's not just words, you've got to use it as best we can as people and as human beings. But just listen to the authorities, do your bit, do what you can and hopefully this will go sooner rather than later and everybody can get back to some sort of normality and look forward to what the future holds.

JUN

2020

After Liverpool returned to full training in May, Henderson spoke to the media about how he had dealt with the Coronavirus lockdown before he then turned his attention to lifting yet another trophy as Liverpool captain...

21st: Everton (PL) A
24th: Crystal Palace (PL) H

What's it like to be back? I imagine very good but also a bit strange at the same time – Melwood but not as you know it…

It's very good to be back, just to see the lads, get out on the pitch and get the balls out. It's been really good to get back. It is a little bit different, of course, but ultimately it's really good to get back and start to get going again.

Is it a case of when you're away from something for so long, you realise how much you miss it?

Definitely, definitely. You miss a lot of things; you miss just playing football, but you miss coming in and seeing the lads, having a bit of banter in the changing room and just everything about it – seeing the staff and people at Melwood. You do miss it quite a bit, so to get the ball rolling again and start to come back in has been big for all of us.

Is there a need to get that little bit of a step up to raise the sharpness as time goes on?

You need to keep the fitness levels as high as you can, and we were given a programme from the club to do, which was really helpful for us to try to keep some sort of general fitness up so when we do come back in we're at a good enough level to start doing the twisting and turning, the longer passing back into it. That's been really good for us and I think a lot of the lads will be at a decent level of fitness so when the time does come where we need to play games, I am sure we will be ready.

I'm guessing, injuries aside, this must be the longest you've ever gone without playing some sort of game since you were a kid?

Yeah, probably. It's been a long time, or at least it's felt like a long time. It has been a pretty long time but like I said, really we've been doing quite a bit of training to keep the fitness levels up. Obviously it was a little bit difficult not knowing when you're going to go back, so you need to tailor it as best you can, which the fitness staff have done unbelievably well for us. We're in a good enough position now to start getting going again, getting the balls out and introducing longer passing and getting the sharpness back, which hopefully won't take too long and we'll be right back at it again.

You're always focused on the next game, but during lockdown have you had a chance to look back at the season so far?

You do reflect a lot more and look back at things, especially with the time we've been sort of off. I haven't so much looked forward, I've actually looked back a little bit more in terms of the season and actually what we've achieved so far is incredible really, as a team. It's more about using that as motivation within training to keep going, because when the time comes we want to make sure we're in the best shape we possibly can be to finish off as good as we have been for all season really. We want to make sure that when the time is right and we do start playing games again, we pick up where we left off and continue to perform at the highest level, which, looking back, has been incredible for a long period of time. No matter what happens up to this point, I think everybody I'm sure would agree that it's been an incredible season so far and how we perform each and every game – bar maybe one or two – the levels of performance have been so high and so good in different ways throughout the season. It has been unbelievable, so I think that'll never obviously change. That's happened and whatever happens going forward, we'll just want to be in the best position for when football does return, in terms of games, that we're in the best possible place to go out there and perform at that same level and continue to do what we had done for a long period of time now.

The strength and conditioning guys look after things from a physical point of view, but is there a role for you as captain in terms of keeping a check on everyone mentally? Lockdown is difficult for everyone, whether you've got your family with you or you live on your own...
I think there has been a lot of contact between ourselves as players, but also as staff as well. We've been doing live sessions online to keep things going and also having a little bit of banter, which is always also important. That's been really good, the lads have been brilliant. It's been difficult for a lot of them I am sure, especially the ones who are living on their own, but they've had full support from the players and the club, which I am sure has helped them and is really important during a time like this.

How will you adapt to playing matches with no fans in the stadium?

It is different, and it is strange, but at times like this you've got to try to adapt. You've got to try to do the best you can, go out there and enjoy playing football. When you were little and you used to play for your school there was no crowd watching then really, so you've just got to enjoy your football and appreciate that we are able to go back to what we love doing. We've got to embrace that and make the best out of the situation that we can. Obviously it will be good for the fans to have some football on the telly to watch, but of course they'll want to get back into the stadium as soon as possible themselves. Hopefully it will be sooner rather than later, but when it's safe to return we all know they'll be desperate to be back at Anfield. But, for the time being, I think just to have some Premier League football on the telly will help them also.

Some people might be getting carried away with Liverpool's league position but is it fair to say you're not one of them?

I don't want to look too far forward in terms of things like that. We are still very focussed and very determined. There's still a lot of work to do and a job to be done. Although we're in a very good position, I still feel that we have got to perform at a high level and finish the season off well. We need to do what we've been doing for a long period of time and that's give everything in every single game. If we do that then I'm sure we'll be able to get over the line. So it's just focussing on the each game, whenever they come along, and the closer we get to the first game behind closed doors, the more the focus will be on getting sharper.

Jordan Henderson

Sunday, June 21st, 7pm
Premier League
Everton 0, Liverpool 0

Line-up (4-3-3): Alisson, Alexander-Arnold, Matip (Lovren 73), Van Dijk, Milner (Gomez 42), Fabinho, Henderson (c), Keita (Wijnaldum 65), Minamino (Oxlade-Chamberlain 45), Firmino (Origi 65), Mane. Subs not used: Adrian, Salah, Elliott, Williams

Jordan's post-match reaction: 'I think we can be a lot better, of course. We know that (but) there were still some positive things that I thought were good. We tried to adapt to the situation but overall obviously we are disappointed because we wanted to come here and get the three points. Every game in the Premier League is tough and each team can be a danger. You look at our next game against Crystal Palace, who performed well on Saturday, so every game we play will be tough. In the final third I think we can be a little bit better and more clinical but we'll get ready now for Wednesday. There are still plenty of positives, a clean sheet and I thought we defended really well.'

Captain's contribution

The ball spent a lot of time in the middle of the pitch in a typically hard-fought derby but Henderson helped his team control the majority of the game. In the end both sides had to be happy with a share of the spoils.

v Crystal Palace
Wednesday, June 24th, 8.15pm

'THE FANS HAVEN'T DISAPPEARED, THEY'RE JUST SOMEWHERE ELSE'

Premier League

I WANT to start by saying I hope all of you reading this are healthy and safe, as are the people in your lives who matter most.

It seems so strange to begin a column in a football programme with those sort of words, but it is a reflection of where we find ourselves at the moment.

Since I last wrote for a home game at Anfield, so much has happened in the world. It is great to again have the opportunity to do this because it means football is back, but it returns in very different circumstances and against the backdrop of a virus that has had an impact on everyone in the world.

During lockdown I listened and read a lot about people using this period to find perspective. I think we all thought about things during this time that before we never had to. The most basic of things.

I was no different and beyond the everyday worries that we all had, it also provided a chance to pause and think about football and what it means to me.

I really hope I never did previously, but I can say with 100 per cent certainty I will never take for granted having the opportunity to play and be involved in this game. Like all players I've experienced injuries in my career but that's no comparison.

Let me be clear, I'm not saying for one second that being denied the chance to play football has been a hardship where anyone should feel sorry for us. If you were to draw up a list of people who've suffered during this time, professional sportspeople would be very low down. And like most things in life, we're at the top where you would list people who are fortunate and looked-after.

But regardless of that, when football is your profession – and after your family and friends, the most important thing in your life – it's had a massive impact on all of us.

Perspective is a key thing for me now we are back playing again. I totally understand that there'll be some people who still aren't ready to get back into following the game, and people – even passionate Liverpool fans – who have far bigger worries and concerns to rediscover the interest they previously had.

If there's one thing the last few months has taught us, it's that in life there are far more important things than the result of a football match and much bigger heroes and role-models than professional athletes.

When we think of heroes now we think of the doctors, nurses, paramedics and ambulance drivers who put their lives at risk to save ours; the workers in hospitals and the care sector who couldn't 'stay home' when we were all told to; aside from the wider health service, the countless others, too, who each morning when people like us were logging on to Zoom or Skype to work, still had to go in, not knowing what they were facing.

I know many of you reading this will fit into the

categories above. It's impossible to put into words how thankful we are, but maybe the best way to express it will be to still remember your importance when life is back to normal.

So, coming back to work as a footballer comes with the perspective of how unbelievably privileged we are. I like to think we all knew this before, but without doubt we recognise it more now. And with this chance to return to work, there comes responsibility.

We know we are fortunate that we are allowed to resume playing and all players will understand we have to show the people watching from home that we appreciate this opportunity.

Of course we all want the fans back as soon as possible, because they make the game what it is. But the fans haven't disappeared – they're just somewhere else. They still watch and they still support.

I really hope the amount of games we play with the seats empty is kept to the lowest number possible, but in the meantime it is not an excuse for less effort and commitment – if anything, it's the opposite. We have to embrace the responsibility of delivering for them, because we have a chance to be in the stadium today and they don't.

We have been very strong in encouraging supporters to put their health and that of others first. For the moment, that means supporting us from home.

Liverpool fans, and in fact the overwhelming majority of football supporters, didn't need a message – they already knew this. The idea that fans of our sport are somehow less responsible than everyone else makes no sense. But the message is there for all of us – players and supporters – to abide by, and we will do so.

I've also read a lot about 'not knowing what to expect' when football returns, but in terms of today I can tell you exactly what to expect: a Crystal Palace side that will be giving everything to beat us. That element will never change.

I'm very lucky to know Roy Hodgson well and he is a brilliant coach and leader. I know and have played with a few of the Palace team. They are unbelievable competitors. They'll want to beat us and we have to make sure we don't allow it.

That part of the game will remain the same. An unbelievably competitive contest where you have to give everything or you get nothing.

Returning to other matters away from the pitch, there are two things I'd like to highlight. Firstly, on behalf of the entire playing squad at Liverpool, a thank-you to our amazing staff at the club for how they've looked after us to get us back to this point.

I'm not going to list names because the column would fill half the programme to get them all in.

But from the coaches to the medical team, to the

operational and administrative staff, we have the opportunity to be back playing today because of their dedication and professionalism, and we will always be grateful.

Finally a topic that has been widely commented-upon by people far more qualified than me: Black Lives Matter. I spoke earlier about being privileged in life and part of that is, I personally have never been the subject of discrimination. But I've seen the impact it has on others and it's right that football has been at the forefront, offering its voice to this movement.

I encourage ourselves and our supporters to read up and listen to those who know how damaging racism in our society can be and also, more importantly, understand what we all have to do to help bring about change.

We can all do more to learn and be better. That has to be the real message and hopefully it has an impact.

Liverpool 4, Crystal Palace 0

Goals: Alexander-Arnold (23), Salah (44), Fabinho (55), Mane (69)

Line-up (4-3-3): Alisson, Alexander-Arnold (Williams 74), Gomez, Van Dijk, Robertson (Elliott 84), Henderson (c) (Oxlade-Chamberlain 64), Fabinho, Wijnaldum, Mane (Keita 84), Firmino (Minamino 74), Salah. Subs not used: Adrian, Lovren, Jones, Origi

There were no over-the-top reactions despite a superb performance putting the Reds within touching distance of winning the Premier League title. Mo Salah crowned his return to the team with a brilliant goal. He said: 'I feel great. Since I came here I said I want to win the Premier League with the team. The city didn't win it for a long time, so it was the right time. Maybe last year we had a chance to win it but Man City also performed really good and they won it. It's our time to win it and it's great. Two points to go to win the league, it's great. We had a great performance today and all the players were unbelievable. I'm happy about the result and looking forward to the next few games. I think all the players are motivated, everyone is motivated in his way – but everyone is motivated to win the league.'

Captain's contribution

Henderson came close to scoring on a night when his team did him proud, proving there were no title jitters as they swatted Palace away with a dominant performance. Jordan was replaced by Alex Oxlade-Chamberlain after 64 minutes but by then the hard yards had been run.

Post-match note: Twenty-four hours later Chelsea's victory over Manchester City confirmed the Reds couldn't be caught at the top. A 30-year wait for the title had ended – with a record seven league matches still to play. The celebrations could begin!

Henderson had made history as Liverpool's first Premier League-winning captain and he reflected on the achievement...

Liverpool are Premier League champions. How does it feel?

Amazing, it's hard to describe to be honest. But after the final whistle [in the Chelsea v Manchester City game] it was just an amazing feeling again, especially to spend it with all the lads and the staff. To finally get over the line is a relief but also an amazing feeling.

What were the emotions like, watching the game unfold at Stamford Bridge?

We were pretty relaxed, just trying to enjoy the game, but then any little bit of action at either end of the pitch, it was a bit tense. There was quite a bit that was happening, especially in the second half, so it was a good game to watch and in the end, obviously we were delighted with the result and hopefully we can start to celebrate once I'm finished here!

You're all there together, how important was that for you, to be able to enjoy that moment together after working so hard for it?

It was definitely important for us to be together I think, in this moment. We didn't know if we were going to watch the game together but I felt like if something did happen, where City drop points and we did win, I felt it was right to be together and thankfully we were tonight and we all can celebrate together.

Was there a point or a game during the season where you thought 'that could be the key moment'?

I know you're probably bored of me saying the next game is the main focus and that's all we focus on, but honestly that is the truth, it was the truth then and it always will be. That is the focus, it's so narrow and you just want to concentrate on each game because that's why we were so successful last year and that's why each game we've been able to be so consistent because we haven't really been thinking about the end goal. We're thinking about that 90 minutes and that team that we're playing against so I think that has worked really well for us. That's not just something I was saying, or the lads were saying, in front of the cameras, that was the truth. We didn't want to think about four, five, 10, 15 games down the line, because you can't change that – all you can change is the next game. And like I say, I felt as though we've done that so far throughout the season really well and now it's another challenge to be able to do it from now until the end of the season.

What about the Manchester United game at Anfield in January, when the fans started singing 'we're gonna win the league'?

There were numerous games where I felt there were big results and big performances in certain stages of the season, but at the same time I never got carried away after a win or a performance – it was literally 'job done, let's pick it up next game and go again and keep doing that until we get to this point'. You never know what is going to happen in football, you can never predict what's going to happen in the future, so you've just got to live for the moment, live for the game and the next game and concentrate solely on that 90 minutes.

In 2014, you missed out by a couple of points. Last year, you missed out by a point. What does this mean to you personally?

A lot! Like you say, I've been close last year, very close, and 2014 I was close again and both [times] lost out to City. So yeah, this does feel really special for me personally but also I'm so happy for my teammates, for the fans, for the club as a whole, because they've been waiting so long for this Premier League title. I'm just so proud to be part of this football club and this group of lads; they deserve it, I know how hard they work every day in training. What we've done over the past couple of seasons, I've felt we've deserved to win the Champions League, the Super Cup, the Club World Cup and now the Premier League. Now it's about keeping that going, staying hungry and keeping going and I've got no doubt that the players here will want to do that.

You went so close last season, how did you manage to not fall away but kick on and be even better this term?

I think you can use that as a motivation and that as extra energy to keep going and to want to do it really, to want to get over the line and finish the job off. Last season we played so well and were so unlucky, but City were amazing and they managed pip us in the end. We kept going right until the last day and that's all we could ask for really. Obviously a few weeks later winning the Champions League helped, and then I think we've kicked on again and we've been unbelievable this season. For now it's about keeping on improving, keeping on doing the things we've been doing to get to this point but also keep improving, learning even more and if we do that then I'm pretty sure there'll be more trophies available to us in the near future.

Finally, what will it mean to you to lift the Premier League trophy? It's been 30 years since a Liverpool captain did that...
I could never in words describe the feeling of winning the Premier League, just like I couldn't describe winning the Champions League. It's a unique feeling and one that, again, I'm very proud of. I've been so honoured to be part of this football club and to go on the journey to be with this manager, this group of players, these fans – it's been so special. But we'll enjoy this, we'll celebrate, but then I know in the next few days they'll be straight onto the next game and finishing the season off as well as we can. We want to win every game and we want to finish off with the highest points record we can and give everything we've got and then we'll go into next season and we'll want even more.

JUL

2020

Liverpool were champions for the first time in 30 years but there was still a season to finish - and an emotional evening at Anfield that Liverpool fans will never forget ...

2nd: Manchester City (PL) A
5th: Aston Villa (PL) H
8th: Brighton (PL) A
11th: Burnley (PL) H
15th: Arsenal (PL) A
22nd: Chelsea (PL) H
26th: Newcastle (PL) A

Jordan Henderson

Thursday, July 2nd, 8.15pm
Premier League
Manchester City 4, Liverpool 0

Line-up (4-3-3): Alisson, Alexander-Arnold (Williams 76), Gomez (Oxlade-Chamberlain 45), Van Dijk, Robertson, Fabinho, Henderson (c), Wijnaldum (Keita 62), Mane (Minamino 85), Salah, Firmino (Origi 62). Subs not used: Adrian, Milner, Jones, Elliott

Henderson was not happy with Liverpool's performance. He said: 'We are not making any excuses. We are bitterly disappointed and we expect more from ourselves but it can be a lesson for us going forward if we want to improve and keep contending for trophies and being in the run-in for the title next season and other competitions as well. We need to keep going, keep improving and keep learning. This is a learning curve tonight so we need to react the right way in the next game. It's never nice to lose games. We need to show our character and again, react in the right way. The next game is Sunday so it comes thick and fast and we need to be ready and keep going.'

Captain's contribution

Henderson was the heartbeat of Liverpool's efforts at the Etihad but the Reds were off the pace against Pep Guardiola's side. One sublime ball through to Sadio Mane again highlighted the range of Henderson's passing.

v Aston Villa
Sunday, July 5th, 4.30pm

'THIS LIVERPOOL WAS BUILT ON STEVIE'S LEGS AND STEVIE'S SHOULDERS'

Premier League

WE'RE back at Anfield today for the first time since clinching the Premier League title.

That's not a bad way to start my column, is it? But we, as a team, also have a clear message: we might have achieved the target we set out for ourselves last summer, but as the gaffer has made it clear, we consider our season far from over.

Quite the opposite, actually. There's as much to play for as there ever has been.

I think it has been a defining characteristic of our team in the past three seasons – and maybe beyond – that we treat every game we play like it is the most important of our lives. I can promise you, on behalf of all the boys, we aren't going to stop that now.

And when you play the quality of opponents we do, it's the only approach you can take. Aston Villa are a brilliant side who gave us arguably one of our toughest challenges all season at their place. Even 99 per cent effort and concentration will mean we'll get beat. So, we have to be on it. We have to be at 100 per cent.

All that said, given what's happened since I last wrote this column, it's impossible not to acknowledge it, even though come kick-off it won't be in any of our minds.

I'm sure when the moment came, when we were mathematically confirmed champions, everyone who is connected to this club immediately thought of someone else close to them. For me, it was my wife and children and my mum and dad. That might be the reason I was seen with let's say 'red eyes' in the TV interviews straight after... But I saw on social media, and in videos, it was the case for many people: players, ex-players and most of all supporters.

When something significant like that happens – and you're lucky enough to be part of it – you do think of those who've helped you get there. The people who made it happen.

I could fill the entire programme listing people I am grateful to and, by the way, none more so than all my current team-mates, the gaffer, his direct staff and the unreal club staff, who we don't get to see as much of. But there are three people whose contribution to me personally here at Liverpool I want to highlight and thank.

Firstly, Sir Kenny Dalglish. One of the things that set me off on the night we won it was seeing Kenny on TV immediately after and how emotional he was. Along with Damien Comolli, to whom I will also be forever grateful, Kenny is the reason I got the opportunity to play for this amazing club.

I can still remember, clear as day, the first conversation we had and the first meeting we had. I still remember those first training sessions.

Sir Kenny taught me how special this club is and that when you are privileged to represent it on the pitch, you carry a great responsibility. I loved every minute of playing for Sir Kenny and he taught me more than I can explain in words.

The gaffer said that Kenny is our 'soul' and that is such a great description. To know he is in the stands supporting us – home and away – drives us on as a team. When he is on our plane coming back from away-games every player wants to shake his hand.

I can never repay what he did for me, but I hope the joy we have bought him on the pitch, in the last few seasons especially, has gone some way to show the gratitude he deserves.

Secondly, is Brendan Rodgers. I think on the outside Brendan probably isn't given the credit he deserves for the role he played in our journey as a club. But I know on the inside, from people who know and understand, it's hugely appreciated. You only have to listen to our gaffer now speak.

When Jürgen says one of the biggest things that attracted him to come to Liverpool in the first place was because it was an outstanding team, in great shape, you realise how important Brendan was.

He made me captain and it was a brave choice. I was young still and I'm sure he could have picked other candidates who were more experienced. Whatever he saw in me that made him think I was worthy of that honour I don't know, but I couldn't be more thankful.

Again, Brendan is a person who invested a lot of time and energy into me as a professional and I learned so much from him and his staff at the time.

Thirdly, is Steven Gerrard. It's impossible to sum up the importance of Stevie to the modern Liverpool and what we are achieving together now. If you speak to every player in our dressing-room – from the oldest to the youngest – they'll all tell you that following in the footsteps of Steven Gerrard was a massive factor in wanting to sign for this club. It was for me, and I was lucky to play alongside him for club and country.

Looking back now, as a player, you cannot get any better education than being in the same team as Stevie. Everything about him was inspirational.

Again, turning to the gaffer's words, this Liverpool was "built on Stevie's legs" and Stevie's shoulders. He is the benchmark for any player coming to this club today. The way he handled pressure. The way he protected the team and the club. The way he led and the example he set. The quality he had. Wow.

When we won the Champions League in Madrid and we went back to the team hotel for the party, someone told me Stevie was in the room. It took me ages to find him, because he was tucked away in a corner. He told me it was because it was the current players' night and he was there as a supporter, feeling privileged to see the lads celebrate.

That sums him up, but whether Stevie likes it or not – for so many of us in this current team – his contribution to what we have achieved can't be underestimated. He set the standards we all work day in and day out to reach. His values and his example drives so many of us on. The club we have today – with the support and the backing – is because of him.

As I said before, there are so many people who play a pivotal part when a team accomplishes something special and there are dozens upon dozens of others I could name here.

And the most pleasing thing for me and many of the current team is that the congratulations and joy from the legends, who built this club, is heartfelt and genuine.

Their joy is real – they all mean it.

On behalf of the current team, I thank all of them for making Liverpool the club it is and giving us a platform to create more memories and stories.

Liverpool 2, Aston Villa 0

Goals: Mane (71), Jones (89)

Line-up (4-3-3): Alisson, Alexander-Arnold, Gomez, Van Dijk, Robertson (Williams 89), Fabinho (Henderson 61), Keita (Jones 85), Oxlade-Chamberlain (Firmino 61), Mane, Salah, Origi (Wijnaldum 61). Subs not used: Adrian, Minamino, Shaqiri, Elliott

Curtis Jones had a week to remember, signing a new long-term deal at Anfield as well as netting his first *Premier League* goal for the Reds. He said: 'I'm just grateful for the manager and the rest of the staff for having the belief in me and putting me out there when it was only 1-0 and Villa were playing well. I'm grateful for that but it's been a good week. He [Klopp] was just saying the usual, he knows that I'm good on the ball but it's about picking the right pass and knowing when to dribble. I think for any young lad that's coming into the team like this, I think you've got to be confident, you've got to be brave and want to get on the ball. That's what I try and do. Growing up, I've always watched Liverpool and there's been some great players, including my idol Steven Gerrard and his team that he played in was great. But I definitely think that this is the greatest I've watched and I'm grateful to be part of it.'

Captain's contribution

Henderson started this game on the bench as Klopp opted to rotate his squad. With just less than half an hour left, he was brought on to try and increase Liverpool's tempo and added plenty of drive from midfield.

Wednesday, July 8th, 8.15pm
Premier League
Brighton 1, Liverpool 3

Goals: Salah (6, 76), Henderson (8)

Line-up (4-3-3): Alisson, Alexander-Arnold, Gomez, Van Dijk, Williams (Robertson 45), Henderson (c) (Milner 80), Wijnaldum, Keita (Fabinho 61), Oxlade-Chamberlain (Mane 61), Salah, Firmino (Minamino 87). Subs not used: Adrian, Origi, Jones, Elliott

Mo Salah's brace was the foundation of this win for the Reds and he revealed that his second goal, a darting, glancing header, was designed and planned at Melwood. He said: 'We trained it yesterday and two days ago - and finally Robbo gave me an assist so I'm happy for that. I think it was a good game for fans to watch. They play really well from the back and they had a good game. We were lucky a bit to score in the beginning twice, [that] made the game a little bit easier to just have the confidence from the beginning. But they played a good game. After I scored the third one it made the game calm again.'

Captain's contribution

Henderson worked his socks off until a knee injury in the second half brought his game to a premature end. He scored a superb goal from outside the box early on and ran the game with aplomb for the Reds.

v Burnley
Saturday, July 11th, 3pm

'THERE IS NO BETTER ENVIRONMENT THAN THE ONE THEY'RE IN RIGHT NOW'

Premier League

IF it's the responsibility of a football club to ensure it looks after its future while protecting its present, then the news that came out in the last week at our place is as positive as it can get.

Within a few days of each other, Curtis Jones and Harvey Elliott committed their futures to Liverpool, although the circumstances were different.

Curtis had only signed a long-term deal about ten months ago, so this new deal was about reward rather than securing his services, but I couldn't be more pleased for him. Everyone knows what a huge talent he is. For me, I saw it in the first training session he had with the first team at Melwood. Ability coming out of his ears.

But I think the gaffer said it himself this week that skill in isolation isn't enough. Football is full of unbelievably talented players, but to achieve your full potential you need more and Curtis has shown he totally understands that.

Sometimes it's the little things that demonstrate how much it means to a player. Do you do the stuff that the supporters don't see? That is just as important.

Things like listening to the coaches and getting in the gym before training, following their plans and engaging with them to find the small margins where you can get an edge. I've seen that in Curtis; he wants to be better every day. And not just with a ball at his feet. In every aspect of being a professional.

It's so pleasing to see how he's grown and developed and sometimes I have to remind myself how young he is, because he has the physical attributes of a much more experienced player. When he scored his goal against Aston Villa you could see immediately how chuffed the other boys were and that's because we all recognise the strides he's made to get to this point.

But the crucial thing now is that he continues doing exactly what he's done to get here. If he keeps that attitude of making sure improvement and learning is his number one focus, he really can achieve anything he wants.

The fact he's a local lad as well only adds to it. I know the feeling of representing the club you grew up supporting and how special that feels. Curt gets that with that comes responsibility and again, you can see he's embraced it and is using it to drive him on.

Not long after Curt's renewal came Harvey Elliott signing his first pro deal with the club. Again, all the boys were buzzing when that was announced.

Harvey is in a very different stage of his development to Curtis, because of his age, but nonetheless the same lessons apply. His talent is frightening. But again, ability gets you so far and then mentality and attitude have to match it.

We've seen Harvey grow as a player and a person during this campaign and what excites me most of all is that there is still so much more room for development. He gets that as well. You can see he has a hunger and thirst for learning from the coaches and from the other players.

You will not meet a nicer, more grounded lad than Harvey off the pitch and he fits in perfectly to the culture we have in our dressing-room. And I think, without sounding immodest, the environment we have at Liverpool is perfect for him.

I think we've shown in recent seasons that our dressing-room has a 'no excuses' culture and I know from my own development as a player how important that is.

Harvey has won the lottery being able to see first-hand what players such as Adam Lallana and James Milner put in away from the pitch, which has allowed them to have the amazing careers they have had.

The other point to make, on Harvey in particular, is to back up something the gaffer said, which is about allowing him space and time to grow. There is quite a lot of focus on Harvey and I get that because of things like being the youngest player to make an appearance in the Premier League. That brings a spotlight and scrutiny that can have an impact.

As a club and as a team we will make sure our environment is protective of these lads. They have to be allowed to make mistakes, have bad moments, because it's from those periods that you learn the most.

Being at a club like ours, at their age, is a challenge and we all have responsibility – players, staff and even supporters – to make sure we have the patience and understanding to help them through the more difficult spells and not add to the pressure. Lighten the load on them, not add to it.

I've focused on Curtis and Harvey purely because they've signed new deals in the past few days, but I could easily have spoken in the same terms about others.

Neco Williams has been incredible for the team in the way he trains and performs. He's a crucial member of this squad now and his development is really exciting. His attitude and application is elite. He goes about his business quietly but on the pitch he doesn't take a backward step. It's been a real pleasure for us to watch him develop this season.

In addition, Leighton Clarkson, Jake Cain and Yasser Larouci have shown superb quality as part of our group. Caoimhin Kelleher likewise with the keepers, he's been brilliant. All of these lads show they understand what is needed to be part of this group and contribute.

Most recently we've had Paul Glatzel back in full training and everyone is made up about that. I don't want to dwell on Paul's setbacks as I'm sure everyone knows the bad luck he had. But a player is defined by how he reacts to these blows and Paul has the mentality that says to all of us he is going to have a big career. He loves to score goals and seeing him back in training and looking sharp is magic.

If anything, Paul epitomises the attitude and character needed. He's an example to a lot of the young players. He has never felt sorry for himself, is committed to making sure he can be the best he can be, and he works as hard as any player I've ever seen to give himself the chance to fulfil his potential. I hope Paul is as proud of himself for how he's conducted himself in the face of setbacks, as we are of him.

If these lads continue to apply themselves each and every day, on and off the pitch, then I believe there's no better environment to be in than the one they're in right now to fulfil their potential.

Liverpool 1, Burnley 1

Goals: Robertson (34)

Line-up (4-3-3): Alisson, Williams (Keita 69), Gomez, Van Dijk (c), Robertson, Fabinho, Wijnaldum (Oxlade-Chamberlain 81), Jones (Alexander-Arnold 69), Mane, Salah, Firmino. Subs not used: Adrian, Lovren, Minamino, Shaqiri, Origi, Elliott

A draw with Burnley meant Liverpool could still beat Manchester City's Premier League points record of 100, set in 2018, and Fabinho was confident the Reds could still achieve that feat. He said: 'Always when we go out onto the pitch, we go to win. We don't look at the opponent, we just go to try to do our best with intensity and technical play. So we go into these three final games to win. It's hard to play against a team like Burnley because they have very good things like [being] very strong on set-pieces and we know we had to have very good concentration. It's like this but you have to find the spaces to try always but today was not our best day maybe. I think in general we played a very good game. We created very good chances to score, their 'keeper Pope made very good saves as well. The intensity was good so unfortunately the result is not a win but we keep going.'

Captain's contribution

The knee injury Henderson picked up against Brighton proved to be more serious than first thought so Liverpool's captain missed this match. It was also confirmed that he would miss the remainder of the season as he looks to recover from the problem.

Wednesday, July 15th, 8pm
Premier League
Arsenal 2, Liverpool 1

Goals: Mane (20)

Line-up (4-3-3): Alisson, Alexander-Arnold, Gomez, Van Dijk (c), Robertson, Fabinho, Wijnaldum (Shaqiri 83), Oxlade-Chamberlain (Minamino 61), Mane, Salah (Origi 83), Firmino (Keita 61). Subs not used: Adrian, Lovren, Shaqiri, Jones, Elliott, Williams

Virgil van Dijk deputised for missing captain Jordan Henderson and was disappointed that the loss meant Liverpool could no longer achieve the 100-point mark in the season. However, he was looking forward to lifting the Premier League trophy with his teammates after Liverpool's next match with Chelsea. He said: 'It will be a dream come true. Being champions of the Premier League is already a dream come true. Obviously tonight the disappointment is what's in my head at the moment, but I go home and it will be all fine. That's the life of a football player: sometimes you win and you be the hero, and sometimes you can be the villain in certain cases. We'll try to win the last two games and get a well-deserved break, but we don't need to forget that we had a fantastic season already.'

July 2020

v Chelsea
Wednesday, July 22nd, 8.15pm

'I CAN PROMISE YOU: WE WILL FEEL YOU WITH US WHEN WE LIFT THAT TROPHY'

Premier League

I HAVE been asked many times since we were confirmed as Premier League champions to sum up how I feel and I'm not too proud to admit I don't think I've produced a good answer yet.

Part of that is because the initial feelings were too overwhelming. Anyone watching the media interviews in the minutes after it was confirmed could see that. Another element is that we still had a job to do and a relatively long wait until this moment this evening.

I think now I can find the right word: gratitude. There are so many different people responsible when a team is successful and as players we are privileged to attract the most attention, the most praise and the biggest rewards. But behind the team there are so many different individuals and groups who make a side successful.

At Liverpool every single player in our dressing-room recognises how fortunate we are to have the best in the world looking out for us and after us – and on a night like tonight it's important to express that appreciation.

The supporters, of course, are a huge factor. Without them this club isn't what it is. Speak to anyone in the world about Liverpool Football Club and the conversation always comes back to the passion and emotion around the club – and that's entirely down to our fans. This is an emotional club and we shouldn't shy away from that fact. It brings pressures, yes, but it means everything we do together means more – in good times and bad.

It's gutting for all of us that our fans are not with us in person today, but we can still make this one of the most enjoyable shared experiences we've ever had if we want it to be.

If anyone reads this column or these words prior to the evening of the match, I cannot say clearly enough it is critically important you stay away from Anfield and enjoy celebrating with us in your own way, at home. The city of Liverpool has been hit hard by COVID-19 and it's important we support our healthcare heroes – the emergency services and key workers – by listening to the advice and staying away from gatherings which aren't safe.

I promise you: we will feel you with us when we lift that trophy, even though you're not at Anfield in person. We are lifting it for you – you've driven us to achieving this dream. But this club's values are about taking care of each other and tonight that means supporting us from home and in safe environments.

Aside from the fans, the other support network we have is the staff who work for this club, specifically the guys at Melwood but also those we don't get to see as often. A club as big as Liverpool can only operate successfully if every employee performs to their highest level. That's what we have here, off the pitch as much as on.

At Anfield, Chapel Street, the shops, LFC Foundation,

community work and other club locations, we have hundreds upon hundreds of staff who go above and beyond to make LFC successful and so support what we do on the pitch. If the club is poorly run, the team has no chance.

Unfortunately circumstance means we don't get to meet everyone we can proudly call colleagues – but it doesn't mean we don't know about the contribution and recognise the significance of it.

The staff at Melwood, of course, we do know personally – and on behalf of all the players I want to take this chance to tell them they mean everything to us. I think I have the best workplace in the country and the rest of the players say the same thing.

Each day we are looked after by world-class professionals who create a culture and environment where players can thrive. Whether it's the coaches, the medical team, fitness staff, the nutrition experts and chefs, the ground staff, the administration people or security...they dedicate their careers to make our team the best it can be.

It is no exaggeration to say that without these people the team would not be what it is. Without them Melwood would feel different and not give us the same energy. I hope everyone there knows how important they are to us and realise this title is as much for them as anyone.

If Melwood is our 'home' from a work perspective,

then the impact of our actual families is something that each and every player will want to acknowledge after we pick up the trophy later.

Of course, the rewards we get as professional footballers means that everyone in our family-circle benefits, but what often isn't seen or reported is the sacrifices made on this journey by the people closest to us.

I can speak from personal experience that without my immediate family, I wouldn't be where I am today. Without their love and support, their understanding, their patience. They see you at your lowest and most insecure and they carry you on their shoulders. Each player in our squad would tell you the same, I'm sure, about their nearest-and-dearest.

I've been very lucky in my life with things that have happened to me, but without doubt the biggest blessing is my family. None of this would matter if I couldn't share it with them and dedicate it to them.

When we win something, the players lift the trophy – but it is the families who lift the players. These moments are just as much about them in our eyes.

And finally, this team. What can I say about this team and our manager? I said my overriding feeling on summing up this season and becoming Champions of England was gratitude. And my appreciation for my team-mates and the Gaffer could not be higher.

It's no secret what this squad thinks of Jürgen Klopp. If you think as supporters you appreciate what he has done for this club, you can multiply that by a hundred for the team. He is our leader – he has set the tone for all of this from the day we walked in.

As I have said previously, and as the manager has said himself, he took over from great foundations laid by Sir Kenny and Brendan, and from players like Stevie. But he, more than anyone in my eyes, is the reason we are here now about to collect this club's first league title in 30 years.

For the players...the lads I share a dressing-room with and battle alongside on the pitch. I can honestly say I view each and every one of them as family. I know they'd do anything for me, and I would do anything for them. That's what we have and we all know we are so fortunate to have it. Being a very good football team that wins is nice. Being a team of brothers who wins is something else. But people do move on and have new challenges to face and enjoy. We will be saying goodbye to two massively important players this summer and both leave with our thanks for what they have done.

Nathaniel Clyne remains one of the best full-backs in England for me and I know wherever he goes next will have won the lottery to get a player of his talent. We all wish him well.

And then Adam Lallana. My mate. One of my best

mates – in life not just in football. Adam is one of the best players I have ever shared a pitch with. Adam is one of the best professionals I have ever shared a pitch with. He is one of the best people I have shared a dressing-room with. His contribution to where we are now cannot be understated. League titles aren't won in just one season – they are a journey.

Adam Lallana set standards that the rest of us worked to reach and as a result this team and club drove forward. No one will miss him more than me. But I know he still has many years left at the highest level, so we will get to see him again, albeit 'ratting' against us and causing us all sorts of problems with his ability and energy.

So to finish, when the trophy is lifted this evening everyone I've mentioned will be there with us on that podium, if not in person, then at least in spirit and mind. Their hands will be on the trophy as well. Our supporters, the staff, our families and our team.

The best things are achieved together. This is a collective achievement and one we should all cherish and enjoy.

Thank you all for everything.

Liverpool 5, Chelsea 3

Goals: Keita (23), Alexander-Arnold (38), Wijnaldum (43), Firmino (54), Oxlade-Chamberlain (84)

Line-up (4-3-3): Alisson, Alexander-Arnold, Gomez, Van Dijk, Robertson, Fabinho, Wijnaldum (Milner 66), Keita (Jones 66), Mane (Origi 87), Salah (Oxlade-Chamberlain 79), Firmino (Minamino 87). Subs not used: Adrian, Lovren, Lallana, Shaqiri

Liverpool finished their home campaign with yet another display of free-flowing, attacking football. Alex Oxlade-Chamberlain, who scored a fine goal at the Kop end, hopes Liverpool's Premier League title win is just the beginning for the Reds. He said: 'We've done really well in the last three years since I've been here and we need to just keep building on it, but it's a good time to be a Liverpool player and to be involved in this amazing football club so I'm really looking forward to what comes next, but we need to stay hungry and stay focused.'

Captain's contribution

As a player, Henderson's season might have been over but after this match he did something no other Liverpool captain has done for three decades; lifted the league trophy. There were no fans inside Anfield but that did not stop Henderson and Liverpool's ecstatic squad and staff from celebrating in a special ceremony in the Kop. After 30 years, the waiting was finally over... and the party could well and truly begin.

LET THE CELEBRATIONS BEGIN...

Relief and ecstasy were the overriding emotions as, almost 12 months after an extraordinary journey began, the footballing world finally got to see a Liverpool captain lift the Premier League trophy. It's a feeling that was hard to explain but Jordan Henderson spoke for all Liverpool fans when he outlined his pride at captaining this extraordinary side...

On the emotions of receiving the trophy...

We've been waiting a long time, like I said before the game. The build-up to it, walking up there was amazing. Like I said, the lads deserved the moment tonight. The families were up there watching, which was a big thing for us as a team. It's been an amazing season and to crown it off like that was really special.

On whether there was one pivotal moment in the season...

Not really. The start was really important, of course. From then, we just grew and grew as the season went on, got stronger, more confident and ruthless really. We found a way to win on so many occasions and that's just down to mentality. The lads have been brilliant all season and they deserve what they get now.

On Liverpool's mentality after missing out on the title by one point last term...

It makes it even more special. After last season, getting 97 points and not winning it was hard to take, but then we reacted a few weeks later and won the Champions League. At the start of the Premier League season we knew we had unfinished business. It's been an amazing season and I'm so thankful that I'm part of this club and part of this team that has managed to get the Premier League after 30 years.

On whether he ever dreamed he would win the Premier League...

I always dreamed, you know. The Premier League has been a

dream of mine since I was a kid and that was one of the reasons why I wanted to come to Liverpool – you want to win trophies and the expectations are so high. But when you come as a young player, it's so difficult. It's been a process, a journey and it hasn't happened overnight. Over the past five years since the gaffer came in, it's been a process, a journey and every single player has been a part of that journey. To finish the season off like this has been really special. We can enjoy tonight but, after this, next season is going to be a big challenge for us. I thought tonight we showed the mentality again to come and perform like we did, and get the result we did.

On the bond among this team...

That's the most important thing – it's a team. Of course, you're going to have individuals that perform but the most important thing is the team. We're always there together for each other, it's a really close group – as you can see – and that's off the field and on the field. It makes a massive difference and it's another thing the gaffer has brought since he's come in: that togetherness in the dressing room. It has made a really big difference on the pitch.

On receiving individual praise for his performances this season...

It's obviously nice to hear good things but, at the same time, it's not really about me. It's about the team. I wouldn't be where I am today without the players I have played with since I've been at Liverpool, the managers that I've had, the coaches that I've *worked with and the team these last few years has been immense and helped me massively. I'm lucky enough to be a part of this football club, lucky enough to work with some amazing people that have helped me. I have always tried to give everything I've got, I've always tried to improve every single season and that won't stop until I finish.*

Sunday, July 26th, 4pm
Premier League
Newcastle United 1, Liverpool 3

Goals: Van Dijk (38), Origi (59), Mane (89)

Line-up (4-3-3): Alisson, Williams (Alexander-Arnold 85), Gomez, Van Dijk, Robertson, Milner, Wijnaldum, Keita (Jones 85), Oxlade-Chamberlain (Mane 64), Minamino (Salah 64), Origi (Firmino 64). Subs not used: Adrian, Fabinho, Shaqiri, Elliott

Virgil van Dijk scored the equalising goal against Newcastle and was impressed with how the Reds came back to end the season with yet another victory. He said: 'It was an outstanding game I think. Second half especially we played amazing football, we created chances and obviously well deserved the win. It's a good feeling to go into a little break and hopefully we'll be good to go and fresh for next season in a couple of weeks.'

INSIDE THE DRESSING ROOM...

After leading Liverpool to glory, Jordan Henderson revealed all about his beloved teammates and manager - and it's clear they have a bond that will last forever...

Henderson on… Alisson Becker

Where do I start?! Ali is the best goalkeeper in the world. I know it is easy for me to say as I play with him but in the big moments, the saves he's made, his distribution, everything about him is world class. He is so laid back off the pitch, so chilled, a brilliant person to have around the dressing room. I couldn't speak highly enough of him really. A top-class keeper and he's made a real difference since he's been at the club.

Henderson on… Trent Alexander-Arnold

The Scouser in the team! I can't say too many nice things about him because I always have to keep his feet on the ground. A great lad who has had an unbelievable season. When you are a young player coming through it is hard to perform. You can have a debut season when you play well as it is all new and different, but I think with the added pressure the following season people expect more from you. He has dealt with that so well. He's been fantastic with the assists he's created but also with the defensive side of things he's worked on too. That has improved massively and he has become a real leader. He is growing and maturing all the time and he has been one of the standout performers in the Premier League this season.

Henderson on… Andy Robertson

Robbo has had another unbelievable season and he's a great lad to have in the dressing room. He gets all the lads going and he has all the banter. He is always there taking the mick out of people, so he's a really good character to have around. But on the football pitch, everyone loves him. He is getting better every year. His energy, work-rate and quality he possesses in the final third. Trent and Robbo are a massive part of how we play as a team.

Henderson on... Virgil van Dijk

I'm going to say good things about the whole team here, aren't I! Virgil is a huge player for us. Everyone knows that. He's made such a big difference since he's been at the club. As a player, as a person, as a leader - everything. I haven't got enough words to describe him. He gives the team confidence and he just gets better and better. A real leader. He is the best centre-half in the world.

Henderson on... Joe Gomez

I can remember when he first came, he had a bad injury and I watched how hard he worked every single day in the gym. I knew one day his hard work would pay off. It is now. He is so good and calm on the ball but aggressive. And I think being next to Virg has helped him. I am sure Virgil will say the opposite though. Another brilliant season from Joe and he can still improve and get better too.

Henderson on... Fabinho

This is getting silly now, isn't it? Another player who has been incredible. Fab is probably one of the best defensive midfielders in the world. He is so good at reading the game and breaking the play up, but also you've seen some of his work in the final third. Some of the passes he has played to create openings have been fantastic. Another great addition to this squad. He has made a big difference.

Henderson on… Gini Wijnaldum

I am a big fan of Gini. I feel as though he is under-rated a little bit. Maybe not from Liverpool fans but I feel as though from maybe outside. As a footballer, he can do everything. He defends, he attacks and can score goals. He keeps it and rarely loses it. For me, a real standout performer who is so consistent.

Henderson on… Naby Keita

I think Naby has grown a lot. It takes some time to develop at this football club, especially if you are younger. Since we have come back from lockdown, his performance level has been really good. Even before then he would be in great runs of form before picking up a little injury here or there that would just knock him back a bit. You can see the talent he has and he can be a fantastic player for this football club. I think people are starting to see the real Naby and what he can do.

Henderson on… Adam Lallana

I think Ads needs to take a lot of credit. When he first came to this club in 2014, he's been a massive part of the direction of change in philosophy to help make this club a success. Anyone who has played with or against him will tell you how good a footballer he is and I am not just saying that because he is my mate. He is a great lad and a great leader in the group and the dressing room.

Henderson on... James Milner

A real big character in the dressing room. He sets the standards every single day, making sure everyone is on it. When he plays, he performs to a high level and he's had a consistent level for so many years. That is so hard to do in the Premier League. The detail he goes in to make sure he is ready for every game and session, it's no coincidence he's still at this level at the age he is at. Definitely the best professional I have ever seen.

Henderson on... Alex Oxlade-Chamberlain

Everybody loves Ox! He's a really likeable character but he's got huge talent and ability as a midfielder. He is really dynamic, he can shoot, he's fast, he's strong and powerful. And he gives us something a little bit different. So I think he has improved again this season. There have been parts of this season where he has shown his quality and he's been fantastic. But still, I think there is still more to come from him in the next couple of years. I think you'll see him get better, improve even more and I am excited to see him improving as he's an exciting player. I have always been a big fan of Ox, I have played with him for a long, long time and I know what he can do. But it is about doing that week in and week out and hopefully that will be very soon.

Henderson on...Mohamed Salah

Another amazing season. People may be critical at times but Mo has been outstanding. He set the bar so high, people expect that every year but look at his performances and his goals, he is incredible. Just look at what he has achieved so far, he has made a huge difference since he came into the club. A great guy off the pitch and a great person to have around. I can't speak highly enough of him.

Henderson on... Roberto Firmino

Bobby! I love Bobby. He is one of my favourite players. He is incredible. Everything about him, I love, really. He's such an important player for this team and a lot of what he does goes unnoticed. He is another world-class player who has had a brilliant season and another who has made a huge impact since he came from Germany.

Henderson on... Sadio Mane

He's been so consistent for a long period of time. An incredible player. I wouldn't like to mark him on a weekend, he is so unpredictable. He can go either way with both feet, so strong and powerful and that doesn't just happen. He is in the gym every day before training doing strength work to get better and improve. I just see that will to improve in Sadio, that desire to get better and take more and that is really important for this team. Yet another standout performer from us in the Premier League. He deserves all the credit he gets.

Henderson on... Divock Origi

Divock is a huge player for us, someone who has had a lot of big moments in this team over the last season or two. He is great to have around and he gives us something different when he comes on. I think he's still young and has a lot to improve on and that is the good thing about this team, we all want to get better and improve, regardless of age or status. I can see that in Div, for sure.

Henderson on... Dejan Lovren

Dejan is a great character to have around. He hasn't played anywhere near as much as he would have liked but he is a big presence in the dressing room. He's missed quite a bit through injury but he is a top centre-half. He's aggressive and good on the ball. He has certainly played his part the last two years. We all love him.

Henderson on... Joel Matip

Joel is very quiet but a great lad, you know. He gets on with his job quietly and efficiently. He is so strong and powerful, it is hard to get around him or past him. You can't win a header against him. He has a really good mentality and he will never be down about things for too long, he can bounce back well. Season was ended early, unfortunately.

And finally... Henderson on... Jürgen Klopp

I could never repay him for what he's given me as a person. But not only me: it's the team really. What he's done since he's come into the football club is so special. So far it's been pretty special, so I just hope it can last for a long, long time and we can just continue to grow, continue to learn from him, and win more trophies.

A FITTING END TO THE SEASON...

Less than 48 hours after lifting the Premier League trophy, Henderson was crowned 2019-20 Footballer of the Year by the Football Writers' Association, a fitting accolade for a man who gives his all for his club ...

An emotional Henderson spoke about his pride at winning the coveted award: *'I'd like to say how appreciative I am of the support of those who voted for me and the Football Writers' Association in general. You only have to look at the past winners of it, a number of whom I've been blessed to play with here at Liverpool, like Stevie [Gerrard], Luis [Suarez] and Mo [Salah] to know how prestigious it is. But as grateful as I am I don't feel like I can accept this on my own. I don't feel like anything I've achieved this season or in fact during my whole career has been done on my own. I owe a lot to so many different people – but none more so than my current teammates – who have just been incredible and deserve this every bit as much as I do. We've only achieved what we've achieved because every single member of our squad has been brilliant. And not just in matches. Not just in producing the moments that make the headlines and the back pages but every day in training. The players who've started the most games for us this season have been as good as they have been because of our culture and our environment at Melwood. No one individual is responsible for that – it's a collective effort and that's how I view accepting this honour. I accept it on behalf of this whole squad, because without them I'm not in a position to be receiving this honour. These lads have made me a better player – a better leader and a better person. If anything I hope those who voted for me did so partly to recognise the entire team's contribution. Individual awards are nice and they are special and I will cherish this one. But an individual award without the collective achievement wouldn't mean anywhere as much to me – if anything at all.'*

SEASON
STATISTICS

Henderson had a season to remember, take a look at his numbers and some of the milestone moments he enjoyed...

Appearances (all competitions)

	PL	FA	LC	CL	Other	Total
Jordan Henderson	30	0	0	6	4	40

Goals (all competitions)

Jordan Henderson	4	0	0	0	0	4

Average passes per game in 2019-20: *75*
Pass completion percentage in 2019-20: *85 per cent*

Selection of milestones from the 2019-20 season:

- *In the 3-1 home defeat of Arsenal in August 2019, Jordan captained Liverpool for the 100th time in the Premier League, becoming only the third Reds player to achieve the feat after Steven Gerrard and Sami Hyypia.*

- *In the 3-1 Anfield victory over Manchester City in November he made his 250th league appearance for Liverpool – the sixth Reds player to do so in the Premier League era.*

- *In the 1-0 home win over Wolves in the final game of 2019, Jordan played his 350th game for the Reds in all competitions. He is now joint-37th on the club's all time appearance list with 364.*

- *Jordan is the 10th different captain to lead Liverpool to a league title following Alex Raisbeck, Don Mackinlay, Willie Fagan, Ron Yeats, Tommy Smith, Emlyn Hughes, Phil Thompson, Graeme Souness and Alan Hansen.*

- *He became the 12th different Liverpool player to be voted the Footballer of the Year by the Football Writer's Association and it was the 14th time a player from the club has lifted the award.*

Final Premier League table 2019-20 season

	P	W	D	L	F	A	GD	Pts
1 Liverpool	**38**	**32**	**3**	**3**	**85**	**33**	**52**	**99**
2 Manchester City	38	26	3	9	102	35	67	81
3 Manchester United	38	18	12	8	66	36	30	66
4 Chelsea	38	20	6	12	69	54	15	66
5 Leicester City	38	18	8	12	67	41	26	62
6 Tottenham	38	16	11	11	61	47	14	59
7 Wolverhampton W	38	15	14	9	51	40	11	59
8 Arsenal	38	14	14	10	56	48	8	56
9 Sheffield United	38	14	12	12	39	39	0	54
10 Burnley	38	15	9	14	43	50	-7	54
11 Southampton	38	15	7	16	51	60	-9	52
12 Everton	38	13	10	15	44	56	-12	49
13 Newcastle United	38	11	11	16	38	58	-20	44
14 Crystal Palace	38	11	10	17	31	50	-19	43
15 Brighton	38	9	14	15	39	54	-15	41
16 West Ham	38	10	9	19	49	62	-13	39
17 Aston Villa	38	9	8	21	41	67	-26	35
18 AFC Bournemouth	38	9	7	22	40	65	-25	34
19 Watford	38	8	10	20	36	64	-28	34
20 Norwich	38	5	6	27	26	75	-49	21

Milestone statistics courtesy of Ged Rea and Dave Ball.